COME

An Invitation to Meet Jesus—Just Where You Are

AS YOU ARE

REUBEN WELCH
DEAN NELSON

Beacon Hill Press of Kansas City
Kansas City, Missouri

10 9 8 7 6 5 4 3 2 1

Contents

About the Authors

Reuben Welch's popular speaking and writing style spans more than four decades and several generations. He joined the faculty of his alma mater, Point Loma Nazarene University, in 1960 and presently serves the school as associate professor emeritus of religion. He is the author of more than 10 books, including the well-known volume *We Really Do Need Each Other.* His roots in the Evangelical and Holiness movements run deep: he is a grandson of the late "Uncle Bud" Robinson. Reuben and his wife, Mary Jo, live in San Diego and are the parents of two grown children.

Dean Nelson is a journalist, editor, and professor at Point Loma Nazarene University. He has authored hundreds of articles, including pieces for the *New York Times,* the *Boston Globe,* and the *San Diego Union-Tribune.* His books include *Heart and Soul: Awakening Your Passion to Serve* and *A New Father's Survival Guide.* Dean lives with his wife, Marcia, and two children in San Diego.

Introduction

$\mathcal{R}$euben Welch is a speaker, teacher, writer, chaplain, and Bible scholar. But few people mention those titles when they talk about him. They use other descriptions: wise, honest, authentic, influential, fearless, insightful, hilarious. But mostly he's bold. For more than 50 years he has spoken and written and helped people see more clearly such issues as the role of Christian community, the reality of temptation, myths about the nature of God, the freedom we have in Christ, and the grace given to us all—and he has said it boldly.

When our hearts are breaking, Reuben shows us that Jesus has entered the pain. When we've lost our way, Reuben shows us that Jesus is the Road under our feet. When we are empty, Reuben shows us that we don't need some*thing*—another experience, for instance—but we need Some*one.*

His books have stood the test of time because they aren't trendy, current only when his substance fits the popular view. His first book (from 1973), *We Really Do Need Each Other,* is as current and important today as it was when it was first published. That's because it doesn't point us to a position. It points us to a Person.

All of the books excerpted here were sermons first. Groups who heard them encouraged him to collect them in book form. In some cases, members of the audience did the collecting and transcribing and made arrangements with publishers.

This volume has something else, though. Reuben and I had a series of conversations about these books—why he wrote them, what drew him to these topics, what was going on in his life when he put them together. They were powerful discussions. I'll always be grateful that we had them. I'm sure restaurants across southern California are still wondering why these two grown men with notepads and books were laughing and crying so much over their breakfasts.

In addition to those conversations, I went through many old sermons of his that weren't published and listened to dozens of tapes of other messages. I was delighted to find that my own collection of Reuben Welch sermons on tape, which covers more than 20 years of my attending his speaking engagements, had survived intact after moves to five different cities.

When word got out that I was working on this project with Reuben, people from around the country offered their own versions of how he had helped them see God and His purpose more clearly. It was similar to what happens when you are considering buying a certain kind of car—suddenly it seems as if *everyone* is driving that kind of car. When I started working with Reuben, I realized that everywhere I went, people had Reuben stories, had Reuben insights, and had been talking about them for years. Only recently had I started paying attention to the influence he has had on so many.

"It's amazing how deeply I have been marked by Reuben Welch," a pastor in Ohio told me recently. He hadn't heard Reuben speak for more than 20 years, but as a student at Pasadena College what he heard from Reuben shaped the kind of minister he is today. There are literally thousands of people similarly "marked."

I'm glad to report that Reuben is still writing, still speaking, still reaching deeper, still inducing tears of insight, still making audiences laugh out loud. But more important, he's still pointing everyone to Jesus.

—Dean Nelson

We Really Do Need Each Other

Dean Nelson

As part of the Sunday morning church service each week, a pastor gave a sermonette to the children of the congregation. They would gather at the front of the sanctuary, and he told them a story—usually from the Bible—that had a Christian lesson to it.

One Sunday, seated on the stairs leading to the platform and surrounded by the children, the pastor began describing a scene in their neighborhood park.

"And something caught my eye as it scampered across the grass," the pastor said. "Can anyone guess what it was?"

The small audience simply stared at him.

"Well," he continued, "it was gray and could climb trees. Anybody know what I saw?"

Dead silence. A few yawns.

Exasperated, he nearly shouted. "Come on—it has a big, bushy tail and gathers nuts for the winter! Can't *anyone* tell me what it was?"

Timidly, one little boy raised his hand.

"Yes! Billy! Thank you! What was it?"

"Well," Billy began, "I'm sure the answer *must* be Jesus, but it sure *sounds* like a squirrel."

Reuben Welch has been a pastor, speaker, author, teacher, and Bible scholar for more than 50 years, and for him the answer to life's complexities, joys, sorrows, victories, and failures have been some kind of variation on little Billy's answer. When it looks as if we have a broken heart, the answer must be Jesus. When it looks as if the circumstances of the day will overwhelm us, the answer must be Jesus. When our achievements appear to cloud our vision of our true purpose on earth, the answer must be Jesus. When our myths and preconceptions about the nature of God confuse us or make us do dumb things, the answer must be Jesus.

I had heard of Christian fellowship before. Wasn't that what the church bowling league was all about? But he was talking about something different.

Reuben's books started appearing in the early 1970s, about the time I first heard him preach. I had never heard anything like what he was saying. He was warm, tender, insightful, and funny.

I still remember the gist of the weekend's worth of messages from God through him. He said that God, through Jesus, creates fellowship within His creation, and that one of the ways we love God is by allowing His presence to change how we interact with one another. In other words, Christ creates community among us where, together, we help each other live as Christians. "We really do need each other," he said. I believe he said this phrase several times over the weekend.

I had heard of Christian fellowship before. Wasn't that what the church bowling league was all about? But he was talking about something different. He was referring to Christ's creating a community of faith where we could confess and encourage and build up one another.

And when the inevitable questions about envy, competition, insecurity, failure, sin, and the like were brought up, he said something like this: What you're describing sounds like a human being. But the answer must be Jesus.

During that first weekend when I heard him speak, when he described Jesus, the One who came *completely* into our experience and condition as human beings, I remembered thinking, "He's describing the most merciful, forgiving Giver of grace I've ever heard of."

Instead of a Sunday School Jesus who leaped off the flannel board and into my heart, I began to discover that love is not what we do for God, but what He does for us. Complete, unconditional love.

Sounded crazy. Must be Jesus.

That was more than 25 years ago. Not long after that we became friends. Just thinking about him points me to Jesus. Throughout the United States and in many other countries, people who have heard him speak remember specific things he says or does during his messages. They remember his insight, his humor, his tears.

They remember his ultimate message because it, like a spiritual compass, always points them to Jesus. Sometimes the turning of the needle itself is memorable. Who can forget the messages when someone gets up and walks out of the auditorium, presumably to cough or something, and Reuben stops in the middle of a sentence and says, "Don't leave now, lady—I promise it'll get better!"

People remember his phrases too. After quoting Eph. 4:7-8, 11, which says gifts are given to some but grace is given to all, he often says, "We really believe that, don't we? No, we don't. Yes, we do. No, we don't. Yes, we do. But we really don't. But we do." He showed us that it is our contradictions that make us human, and that being human is OK.

People remember he was the first to coin the phrase "I think I think"—which means the same, I think, as "I think."

But while he makes most audiences laugh and cry and understand Jesus, not everyone has been moved by his insight. A considerable number have been threatened by his message over the years. No doubt this comes from Reuben's belief that God doesn't fit comfortably in a doctrinal dimension when His nature is revealed in Jesus. The edges around God are harder to describe and define. Reuben, more than anyone I know, is comfortable using fewer words to describe God. He is more comfortable pointing to the life, words, and accounts of Jesus.

People remember Reuben's authenticity about his doubts, feelings of insecurity, failure, and weakness. His honesty about God's strength was magnified in those raw emotions. People remember hearing that the gospel doesn't tell them to "try harder." The gospel, according to Reuben, is communicating that Jesus has made grace available to all.

People remember hearing that the gospel doesn't tell them to "try harder." The gospel, according to Reuben, is communicating that Jesus has made grace available to all.

The Christian life is not a thing to know and to figure out, in Reuben's view. It's a relationship, a journey, with the One who created the world—including us—and who showed us His nature by sending Jesus to love us, to live among us, to die that we might be brought back into right relationship with God once again.

"The biblical perspective of having a personal relationship with God through Jesus is that it's not something you get, but Someone you come to know," he said.

And it's not just God whom we come to know. It's each other too. That's one of the ways we experience God—through the community of believers. It is a relationship that is lived out every day. With each other. Through each other. Because of each other.

He started preaching about this during chapel at Pasadena College in 1968, at a time when the United States was fractured and factioned. So was the Body of Christ, but that part wasn't unique to that era. Many of the dominant religious influences of the day were vehemently preaching about sin and repentance. Reuben took a different approach.

"Why do people remember my granddad?" he asks. His grandfather, known as Uncle Buddy Robinson, died in 1942 at the age of 82 and was famous for his Will Rogers type of uncomplicated insight into God, Scripture, and human nature.

"They remember him because he loved everyone. And somewhere I began to pick up on the idea that repentance comes after grace."

Likewise, he asks, why are people drawn to Jesus?

Sinners don't live their lives pondering how distant they are from God, he said. So what evokes a sense of repentance from them? The awareness that they are loved completely, that God comes to them through Jesus—now, as they are, not as they should be. They don't have to do anything first. God did all the initiating. The journey began before they accepted Jesus, as God came into the world through Him.

"This messes up those who have the system wired—the ones with certainty," Reuben says. "God is a thing, and Jesus is a thing, and being a Christian is a thing, and sin is a thing." Then tears fill his eyes, and he pulls out a handkerchief. I'm convinced he'd be struck dumb if he couldn't let his tears help communicate his point. "Where does that leave the rest of us who *don't* have it wired?"

He doesn't ask that question because he wants to make the weak, confused, insecure, doubting folks feel better. He asks because he knows he really doesn't have this Christian life figured out himself. How does a person explain how God works when that person's daughter is in an institution and needs constant attention? Reuben and Mary Jo's daughter, Pamela, was born with damage to her brain, heart, and central nervous system. Her needs exceeded what her parents and young brother and sister could give her. Her condition was outside the system that others had "wired." She didn't fit. Her lack of recovery didn't fit. Unheeded prayers for healing didn't fit.

Reuben's system was broken. Human.

He thought differently from many of the dominant preachers at that time (as well as the present), in part from his grandfather's influence and in part from his experience with Pamela. It made him think differently about weakness—and sin.

But the language of "being saved," when spoken by many preachers of the day, usually came through as a thing that involved "starting over." It was inconsistent with Reuben's own experience. For instance, as a pastor in Long Beach, California, he began the practice of memorizing Scripture. One particular day he was trying to memorize the eighth chapter of Romans.

"Walking around that church, rehearsing the verses, my heart was saying, 'Father.' I didn't do that. It was the Father. The witness of the Spirit is *Abba!* **Father!** (v. 15). I knew at that moment I was saved. But it didn't mean a new beginning. It meant a holy continuation."

An extension of that experience occurred when he was chaplain, years later, in Pasadena. It also involved the Book of Romans, where he had "a painful/wonderful transition away from old categories and doctrines, to a new language and understanding of grace." He goes so far as to say that this was his conversion experience. Another one. In his office in Pasadena. Already chaplain of a Christian college and professor of biblical literature, he was converted. Again. For him, conversion couldn't be a thing. It was an awareness that he had plunged deeper into his relationship with God. No starting over, but further taking on the new nature.

"It was a shift away from using the Bible to support a doctrine, to coming under the Word of God, and letting it be just that," he said.

Since his own experience didn't square with the sermons that focused on guilt, sin, and repentance, he is sensitive to those in an audience who aren't helped by those kinds of sermons. An evangelist would speak at the college with the aim of having a "great revival" and tell the students that they needed to repent, and later that day the hallway outside of Reuben's office would be lined with students who felt ashamed that nothing had happened in their hearts during the services.

"They heard 'repent,' and that there was something wrong with them if they didn't, and I had to tell them that they'd probably be OK after all," he said, shaking his head.

Standing in the doorway of that office 30 years later, he says, "I'm beginning to remember little trivial things here—but maybe they're really pivotal."

> *"I believe it is acts of grace that draw us to the Father, not accusations."*

Like the time after a "great revival" that a student came into his office and said she would be dropping out of school because apparently she wasn't a Christian, as she previously thought she was. She didn't *feel* like a Christian, the way many in the audience did, she thought.

"I believe it is acts of grace that draw us to the Father, not accusations," Reuben said.

A few years ago, after speaking several times in a large church, he was gathering his notes at the podium and a person approached him.

"I finally figured you out," the man told Reuben. "You operate under the assumption that people are doing the best they can."

"I guess I do," Reuben replied.

"But they're not," the man said. He felt that Reuben was letting the crowd off too easily.

"I guess it's a combination of genetics and theology that keeps me from doing what that man thought I should be doing," Reuben said. "I simply can't condemn. There are some things that won't come out of my mouth."

This is why the study of 1 John became so important to him. Instead of finding ways to accuse members of the Body of Christ, Reuben was drawn to a book that *affirmed* the Body by showing them how to love and live as Jesus lived.

He began to preach in the college chapels about what creates Christian community—that it is our shared life in Jesus.

"What makes us one is not that we do what the college wants or that we fulfill our church founder's dream, but that we share a common life of Christ," he said. "It isn't that you do what I want you to do, but that we have a life together in Jesus."

The themes throughout 1 John are that God loves us and gave us the capacity and desire to love one another, and that when we do love one another, we love God—God dwells in us when we love.

The messages he preached during that school year might have been the end of it, but a colleague, James Jackson Sr., approached Reuben and asked the golden question: "I hear you, but what does it mean?"

The question gave Reuben pause.

"Here I had just given this great illumination on love, and I hadn't thought beyond it," he said. "So I went back to 1 John. I went back to see what it was. What does it mean to love? To live in faith and confession with one another? Is it even possible?"

And amid the other assumptions about what it is to be part of a Christian college, he wondered what could happen if that campus community became a community of Christian love—the type described in 1 John. It drew him into a major conclusion: Life in Jesus is meant to be lived out together, in a community. We learn to love in that community. We love that community. God's love is not to be lived alone. We need each other in order to live as Christ calls us to live.

"I worked on this concept, and it worked on me," he said.

He preached from it again for most of the following school year. He spoke about believers needing to bring their fragments, disillusionment, insecurity, loneliness, weakness, doubts, bitterness, guilt, and love together in a community of human beings who have real human emotions.

He talked about fellowship with those whom God has brought together. He articulated the difference between Christian fellowship and the fellowship of Christians.

"Christian fellowship is when Christians are together being who they are," he said. "It is when they are together sharing, reading, praying, doing what Christians do. And the symbol of the Lord's Supper becomes more meaningful in that experience."

In the context of a Christian college, he could preach this message. The first few messages he preached from the front, with a podium, and the students sat in neat, even rows. But the further they explored this message of a loving Christian community, the closer Reuben moved to them. The rows evolved so that students faced each other. And they lingered longer after the services concluded.

"At any point during the sermon I could say, 'Does anyone need to be prayed for right now?' And we'd stop and pray and confess and love one another," he said. "We were deeply affected by 1 John."

But the students weren't the only ones. In 1971 Reuben was invited to speak at the John T. Benson Company's employee retreat in Nashville. He spoke out of 1 John. He talked about bringing our broken selves before one another in confession and faith. He talked about how our lives in God through Jesus bring us together and create a shared life of fellowship, in the depth of our humanity, at the point of our deepest need and hurt, exploding the myth that there are haves and have-nots in the faith, declaring that we are all have-nots and empty.

He talked about refusing to keep starting over when he failed, but, in forgiveness, continuing to walk in the cleansing, redemptive light of Jesus, the Way, and how that is done in Christian fellowship. He talked about how it isn't as valuable to God for us to tell Him we love Him as it is to believe Him—really believe that He loves us—and that the best way for us to love God is to consciously, intentionally, love each other.

He concluded the retreat by telling them that the strong can't say to the weak, "Try harder," and the weak can't say to the strong, "I can't make it." But to live in Jesus' love they all need to say, "We really do need each other."

Bob Benson Sr., who was running the company at the time, told Reuben that he would like to make those messages into a

book. Benson had recorded them. So the messages were transcribed and sent to Reuben.

Reuben originally put the words on the page the way they
appeared on his own handwritten notes—all over the place, leaving plenty of room on a line for a word that needed to be looked
at slowly and intentionally. But he also did some editing, taking
out the humorous asides, the smart-aleck remarks—"the dumb
stuff," as he called it. Bob called him and said, "You took out all the
good stuff!" So it's all back in the text.

In this compilation of Reuben's works the text is reformat-
ted, but the words are still from the original books that moved
and influenced thousands, and the message is still clear. It's what
he was preaching when I first heard him speak. As you read ex-
cerpts from that first book and his others in the following pages,
I'm confident you'll see something that looks like Reuben Welch
—but because of its wisdom and insight, it must really be Jesus.

Reuben Welch

A Parable

At school a few years ago there was a summer
school course in "Group and Interpersonal Relations."
About a dozen people took the class, and at the end
of it they decided they wanted to do something together as kind of closing to the class. You know, they
had come to know each other, and to share each other, and really be personal to each other, and break
down walls, and so forth. So they decided to get together and take a hike up to Hennigar Flats.

Now, Hennigar Flats is about three miles up the
side of the mountain behind the campus, and it takes
about an hour and a half for anyone to make the hike.
So they set the day and made the sandwiches and
made the chocolate and brought the cold drinks and
the backpacks, and they got all gathered up for the safari, and they started up the mountain—together.

But it wasn't long until the strong, stalwart ones
were up in front, and the other ones were back in the
middle, and way back at the end of the line was a girl
named Jane who was, you might say, out of shape. At
the front was Don—a big, strong, former paratrooper.
He and some others—the strong ones—were up in
front, and the weak ones were back in the back, and
way in the back was Jane.

And Don said (it was he who told me the story)
he looked back a couple of switchbacks and saw Jane,

17

and the Lord told him that he had just better go back
and walk with her. *That's kind of hard on him because he has a need to be first.* But he went down and
started walking with Jane, and the people in the level
above called down, "Come on up. It's great up here."
And Jane yelled, "I don't think I can make it." And they
hollered, *"Yeah,* you can. Try harder; come on up." And
every time they called to her, down went her own
sense of worth, down went her own sense of value.

"I can't make it." "Oh, yeah, you can. Come on." So
the strong went on ahead, and the weak hung behind,
and here was Jane—and she never made it to the top.

Now, look what you have. You have a group—we
know each other, we like each other, we want to do
this together. Let's go to Hennigar Flats together. But
before long, you have divided the strong and the
weak—the haves and the have-nots and the ables and
the unables.

So what started out as a group has now become
a fragmented collection. And so the strong say, "You
can do it." And the weak say, "No, I can't." And so the
strong say, "Try harder"—which is a big help. That's a
big help. And she didn't make it.

Thankfully, that's not the last chapter. They must
have learned their lessons because they decided that
was no way to end the fellowship of that class, and
they got together and decided to do it again. But they
made some new rules—it was everybody go or nobody goes, and they were all going together.

So they set the day and made the sandwiches
and made the chocolate and brought the cold drinks
and the backpacks, and they got all gathered up for
the safari, and they started up the mountain. It took
them four hours to make it to the top, and the water
was all gone and the cold drinks were all gone and
the sandwiches were all gone and the chocolate was
all gone and the backpacks were empty, but they all
made it, together.

Let me share with you the thing that this real-life parable has been saying to me: we have got to go together. Christian fellowship is no place for get in or get out—it's get in, get in. And if you need to slow down, you slow down. That's why it's good for us to read Scripture and sing hymns together; the slow folks have to speed up and the fast folks have to slow down, and we have to do it together.

I know, don't you, that it is God's intention that we go together as a body. It doesn't help much for those who have made it to say to us weaklings, "Try harder. See—I've done it, so you can make it." That makes me think of some dear old grandmother whose children are all gone, who spends all day praying and listening to holy records, saying to a young mother who is going out of her mind with little kids and noise, "Oh, honey, just get alone with God." *Yeah, thanks a lot. You can't even get alone in the bathroom anymore.*

You know something? We're all just people who need each other. We're all learning, and we've all got a long journey ahead of us. We've got to go together, and if it takes us until Jesus comes, we better stay together, we better help each other. And I dare say that by the time we get there, all the sandwiches will be gone and all the chocolate will be gone and all the water will be gone and all the backpacks will be empty. But no matter how long it takes us, we've got to go together, because that's how it is in the Body of Christ.

On Community

Christians are not brought together because they like each other, but because they share a common life in Jesus and are faced with the task of learning how to love each other as members of the family.

I'm sure you could not believe there is ever any

tension in our home. There are four of us who live there. We have three children—two at home. We don't live there at our house because we just met on the street one day and decided we liked each other and decided to take up living together. We live together because we are a family, and sometimes in the midst of the strife and tension and stress what holds us together is not the happy fellowship and congenialities but the fact that we are a family. And because we are, we're faced with the continual task of learning what love means. What brings us together is not our mutualities and congenialities and common interests and hobbies. It is not our mutual esteem or our happy hormones. It is our blood ties, our common name, and our common commitment—it's our parentage and our heritage and our bloodline and our life.

And I think that is apt for the church. So often we say, "You ought to come to our church—you'd like us. You'd like our preacher, you'd like our music, you'd like our youth program, you'd like our golden-agers, our 50-plusers, you'd like us. Come, please come, do come—you'd like us. You'd like us." And if they come and like us, then well and good. But if they don't like us, they spin off and we say, "Oh, too bad. They just never did seem to fit in, did they?" But you see, the church is not the society of the congenial; it is a fellowship based on common life in Jesus. It is the will of God that the Chris-

> *We have talked about personal salvation and individual salvation and "me" and "my" and "my inner life" until we have almost isolated ourselves.*

tian life be lived in the context of a fellowship of the shared life.

When I read that back, it really doesn't seem so profound, but that really has been changing me. I am at a time of emphasis upon the fact that God has made us in such a way that we really do need each other—and maybe I am reacting against what seems to me to be an overemphasis on individualism in Evangelical Christianity.

Some of us are so Westernized and individualized and Evangelicalized that we have forgotten how much we really need each other. I think people like you and me are grossly overindividualized. I think we have talked about personal salvation and individual salvation and "me" and "my" and "my inner life" until we have almost isolated ourselves. And so we just get the idea that it's my life and God's life and you have your relationship to God and I have my relationship to God and of course we ought to be nice to each other and love each other, but what really counts is "my relationship to God."

We Christians act as though we are deep-sea divers. Here we are in the murky waters of sin—but we have the protection of the diving suit of God and we have the lifeline that goes to the great white ship up above. You have your life in Christ and your lifeline and I have my life in Christ and my lifeline and here we are with all our lifelines going up. And we say to each other, "How's your lifeline, brother, you got any kinks? Get it straightened out, keep the oxygen going, or the murky waters of sin will come rushing in on you." We wave to each other and write notes to each other and we bump each other around and we say to each other, "Get your lifeline right." But here I am all by myself. Once in a while someone gets the bends and we bump him up to the top or just cut him off and let him drown.

That's not the way it is—because our life that we have with God is not just my life and His—*no way.* I know this vertical relationship is fundamental. I know that what constitutes us as a community is His life given. I'm not saying that our relationship to God is not personal and unique. I'm saying that we are overindividualized. You know what I'm doing; I'm exaggerating—*but not very much.*

The vertical line of Godward relationship and the horizontal line of human relationship are not two lines but one line in a continuum. It all belongs together. I'm not talking about what ought to be or what would be nice if it were—I'm talking about God's reality about the way He has constituted the life we have with Him. Our life with Him is tied to, is one with, our life with our brothers and sisters. Like the old song says,

You can't have one without the other.

There are a couple of ideas going around in my mind here, and one of them is this isolation thing—this overindividualization that we have. When we feel like we are slipping spiritually or growing cold or indifferent, we have a tendency to withdraw and pray through or to get hold of God or get back to where we ought to be so we will have something to give to others—and that's false.

That separates the full and the empty, the haves and the have-nots; we are all have-nots, we are all empties. Somebody said, "Real witnessing is one beggar telling another beggar where to get bread." We are all beggars—we don't have anything but the life of Christ, and His life in us is not separate from our life with one another.

And I think we are helped in this feeling of isolation by the songs that we sing. I'm thinking of the old song that tells us that on the "Jericho road" there is room for only "Jesus and me." I live at school, you know, and I think the only time that song is appropriate is on a Friday night in the dorm when everybody else is on a date. Then that's a good time to sing, "Jesus and me."

Sometimes the answer to your weariness and heavyheartedness is not to "tell it to Jesus alone" but to begin to share and care with someone else.

Of course there is truth in this and other similar songs. Of course we believe in the total adequacy of Jesus Christ to meet the total need of the total person.

But we must remember this also—He saves in the context of the community of faith. It isn't "Jesus and me"—it is "Jesus and we," and on the Jericho road there is room for Jesus and the whole redeemed community. And if you are like me, when you are burdened and weary and sad, you need Jesus; but you also need someone to be Jesus to you—someone to bring His healing presence to you. And sometimes the answer to your weariness and heavyheartedness is not to "tell it to Jesus alone" but to begin to share and care with someone else.

You can get yourself in a little spiral of self-pity, and so you tell it to Jesus alone and increase your self-pity and your martyr complex. *"Lord, I'm so persecuted, but Lord, You understand." Way to go. That's enough to bless this dying world, isn't it?*

Well, let's go on singing the good songs—it's OK. They aren't true, but it's OK. You see, we really do need each other, not because of the inadequacies of God, but because this is the way His grace works.

I remember a student at school who just before he was to graduate had to go into the hospital with cancer—and he died. He was 22, and he was a ministerial student. Frank Carver, head of our department, and I were very close to him, and we went out to see him and had long talks with him about life and death and God. He knew what was happening, and he said, "You know, I know that God has worked in the past, and I know that God will be with me when I cross the river. I know He will be there; it is those times in between that sometimes are rough."

Do you understand that? Sure you do, and so do I. I know God has been with me, I know God will be with me in the crisis, but here I am right now. He said, "I just wish I was conscious of His presence at all times, like now when I need it." And Frank said to him, "You know, Jesus comes to you in the persons who come to you." Now that is true. Have you experienced that? I have. *It is also true that people can bring the devil, and sometimes we're more familiar with that.* But once in a while someone comes and brings Jesus to me. God has made us this way. We really do need each other.

The point of the passage here, I think, is that Christians are to recognize this reality. John was calling them back to the fundamentals because the fellowship was being threatened, as it still is. How is it healed? By coming back to the great realities that constitute what we are—the life that we have in Jesus is a shared life. Early Christians were often together around those things that made them what they were. They often met together to express their oneness in Christ—around the teaching, around the Word, around the sacraments, and around prayer. They were being together as Christians, not just Christians being together.

I think this is more than playing with words.

There is a fundamental difference between the fellowship of Christians and Christian fellowship. Too often we are together as Christians doing the things we like to do together—volleyball, parties, teas, leagues, receptions, and whatnot. Or we get together and talk about cars and sports and babies and clothes and weather and Sunday School attendance, and we come away having talked and laughed and enjoyed ourselves—but strangely empty and lonely and a little bit guilty. It does not deepen the oneness of the fellowship to multiply such activities. These things do not express our oneness, but the study of the Word does, the sacraments do, and prayer does. We need to be together more, doing the things that really give expression to the common life we share.

You know the best symbol of all this—the Lord's Supper. I have a mental image about the Lord's Supper. I see a table in the Upper Room; *can you see it?* Jesus is at the head of the table and the disciples around the sides. And then I see the wall open up, and the table begins to lengthen. And it lengthens out through the first century and the second century, and it comes all the way into our world to where we are.

Jesus is at the head of the table and all the believers of all the ages are gathered at the table and we are one at one table with the Lord. What is it that makes us one? We share that broken, given life, and so we come and we are one.

There is a beautiful phrase in Gal. 2:9 that expresses this. Paul and his company had gone out from Antioch into the Gentile world, and the saints in Jerusalem were insecure because the "general board" hadn't approved it. But they had gone out on their own and they were coming back somewhat anxiously, and the church gave them **the right hand of fellowship.** It meant that across the prejudices, across the hesitancies, across the insecurities, across the normal barriers that would have separated them, they reached out and said, "God bless you—here is my hand."

And I tell you this—if somewhere in this world there are people who are sharing the life of Jesus together and who are helping each other and suffering with each other, that's my crowd. Those are the people—that is the community of which my heart yearns to be a part. And the name of it is the Church, the Body of Christ, the fellowship of believers.

On Lived-Out Love

I really need to believe that God is not so much concerned that I emote toward Him as that I act in love toward you and believe that He loves me. I think that God is more concerned that I believe He loves me than that I love Him. And that I express that trust in His love by deliberately, consciously loving my brother.

And don't forget that "brother" means fellow Christian. Of course, we are to love all those who come into the circle of our world, but the place where love is to be going on is in the community of believers who share in the life of Christ. If love is not going on between us who know the Lord, what good is talk about loving people "out there"? It doesn't mean anything anywhere if it doesn't mean anything here among us in the fellowship. The Spirit won't let us generalize this too much. John is not talking about a spirit of goodwill toward mankind. He means love to real, live people, beginning with our Christian brothers and sisters right here in the fellowship.

Here is another insight that has been changing me. It has come from hearing John say, "When you say love, think Jesus." It is not enough to say, **God is love** (1 John 4:8, 16). The Bible doesn't end there. You can take that statement by itself and make it a foundation stone on which you can build just about any kind of religion you want. Christian Science is built on the idea "God is love." Buddhism, Hinduism, universalism, humanitarianism can all be built on "God is love." That's not a Christian statement standing alone. Here's the Christian statement: **God so loved the world He sent His Son so that we might live through Him** (see v. 9).

When the Bible says **God is love,** it does not mean God has a general benevolent feeling toward mankind and has opened many roads toward which we may struggle to find Him. It means that God has given himself to us in Jesus Christ. The defining act of the love of God is the coming of Jesus. The word "love" needs a definition, doesn't it? Jesus is the "lived-out" word.

I read a beautiful thing once; I wish I'd thought it myself. I love to get good quotes and never put down where I got them until pretty soon I think I thought them up myself. "The word 'love' needs a dictionary, and for Christians the dictionary is Jesus Christ. He took that chameleon of a word and gave it a fast color so that ever since it has been lustered with His life and teaching—dyed in the crimson of Calvary and shot through with the glories of Easter morning."

Isn't that great? *That should be in the Bible; some scribe just missed it.*

When we say "love," we can mean anything. There are big words in Greek for love—*eros, philos,* and *agape. Eros* is the love of desire—not only love of sex and lust but also love that seeks to own, to possess, to have. A man says, "I just love oranges." If the orange could speak, it would say, "You don't love me—you just want to squeeze me!" I love paintings, I love antiques or music or books—which mostly means I want to have them.

There's another level, *philos,* from which we get
words like Philadelphia—the city of brotherly love—
and fellowship. We have in common, we give, we receive, we share. This is beautiful love and is God's precious gift to us, but this is not the love that John is
talking about. He is talking about love that thinks Jesus in the loving.

Agape love—which is not simply giving love but
giving love in the context of God's sending His Son.
Now, I don't want to run this in the ground, but when
you say love, think Jesus. That's the Christian view.

By "love" we do mean more than a benevolent
spirit toward mankind. That makes me think of another good quote I read somewhere: "It's a shame that in
the minds of so many, the Christian religion has been
identified with pious ethical behavior together with a
vague belief in God, suffused with aesthetic emotion-
alism and a mild glow of humanitarian benevolence."

Isn't that great? *Or perhaps awful.* That makes
you think of a nice pastor in a nice church preaching
a nice sermon to a nice congregation telling them to
be nicer—"the bland leading the bland." That is not
what the New Testament means by love.

"Love" is a strong word. It does not mean total
tolerance or universalism. It means that when we say
"love," we are thinking of Jesus. We are sharing His
love—not mutuality, not congeniality, not what you
have in real neat service clubs plus the inspiration of
the Holy Spirit, not mutual affection plus blessing. It
expresses itself in that love that comes from Jesus
Christ.

What is it that makes it possible for people to
have long, enduring, deepening, close, affectionate
friendships without growing sordid, without wife
swapping, without it becoming unclean and adulterat-
ed? I know we have our troubles and every so often

somebody runs off with the wrong somebody. But what is it that makes it possible for couples and families and friends to love each other, reach out to each other, and touch each other for years and years and years without its becoming unclean or sordid—not denying chemistries or vibrations or potentials, not denying temptations or possibilities?

Here is another life-changing insight for me that is both old and new: Love is commanded.

How can we be friends for long periods of time and it still be good and wholesome and rich and beautiful and supportive? Because the love of Jesus strengthens us. Something very precious happens when we say in Jesus, "I love you." His love is always healing, cleansing, lifting, preserving. It is a good word—because Jesus gave it a fast color.

Here is another life-changing insight for me that is both old and new: Love is commanded. Some things cannot be commanded, and we think love is one of them. But right here it says just as plain as day: **And this commandment we have from him, that he who loves God should love his brother also** (1 John 4:21).

We are commanded to love one another. You see, it has to move suddenly out of the realm of attraction. There are some people that we like, and then there are the other kind. And some who like us and some we can't understand. Now look—if Christian love is restricted to those we have a natural warm feeling for, we have limited our world to the little group we happen to be around. But love is commanded, and if we are going to talk about love, we have to move out of the level of liking and emotion and feeling and warmth to the level of the will—a posture, a stance, an attitude, a frame of mind, a life's direction toward others that's conditioned by our understanding of God's self-giving in Jesus.

We are commanded. It isn't as though we had any alternative. Have we accepted that yet, do you suppose?

I think it is time to get more practical—and maybe time for a word of review. We have been saying that the life of God that Jesus brings into our world is a shared life. God's love for us that "comes down"—the vertical line—is to be expressed through the horizontal line of our personal relationships. God's love for us is defined by the giving of His Son, Jesus, and love for each other is defined by Him too. Our love for each other behaves like Jesus.

Let me try to put some handles on all this talk about love to help us pull it down into the flow of daily life. I'm sure that what I'm going to say now is in First John somewhere. You may have to look between the lines and in the margins, but surely it is there. Love that behaves like Jesus means care for persons as persons. We are to see persons in a personal way, not in a "thingy" way. We have a tendency to put people into categories—that's "thingy" that "thingizes" them; it turns them into "its" instead of "yous."

You know how Southerners are. I do 'cause I'm not one. You know how Westerners are, you know how the Mexicans, the African-Americans, the Asians are. Put them into categories, slip them into little slots categorized, depersonalized, massed-up, and that's not love. Love sees the person.

I never will forget one afternoon when I was coming back from a retreat up in the Sierras. I was taking the back way home, and there were about four or five cars coming down the mountains. It was back of Fresno out in the hot valley, and it was about 110 degrees, and we took a kind of a back road and they were doing repair work on it. And we were just cruising along there, and a patrolman pulled us over. Five of us, and it was just dumb. Here we were 50 miles from nowhere—five irate drivers and this young officer. There we stood in the boiling sun mad as could be at the injustice of the whole thing. And right in the midst of all my disgust I looked at this young patrolman—and he was young—and he was writing out tickets to five angry drivers, and he was trembling. *That was one of my better days.* He was writing with nervous hands, and the creases of his pants were just shaking. And suddenly my whole attitude changed—not that he was right, but it meant my whole relationship to him changed because suddenly I saw him as a young policeman nervous as could be, wanting to do it right and probably wishing he could let us go. But there he was—caught and trembling and nervous, and suddenly I knew how he felt. Behind the uniform was a real, live person.

It's kind of an awesome thing, isn't it? Suddenly my own guilts are rising. We all know those people who fade into the furniture—you know, you don't hear them, you don't see them, you don't know they are there. But I've learned a few things the hard way, and one of them is that there isn't anybody who is a nobody. Everybody is a somebody, and everybody is a "real live people"—with real hopes and real dreams and fears and longings and desires.

I've learned a few things about myself lately. I'm really very sensitive. It took me a long time to accept that. But I am—I'm sensitive as I can be. I think I might make a good pastor if there weren't any such things as votes. I "loves" them contracts. And I can't stand votes—I think they're of the devil. But I know I'm sensitive and I'm probably half neurotic about it. And on the heels of that newfound knowledge has come another fascinating discovery—everybody is sensitive; there isn't anybody who's not sensitive.

"Oh, you know so-and-so—you couldn't hurt him. It runs like water off a duck's back." Oh no, it doesn't.

Did you know that skinny people are sensitive, that fat people are sensitive, that hairy people are sensitive, that bald people are sensitive, and tall people are sensitive, and short people are sensitive? Everybody is sensitive. Love says I care for you as a person. Love says in word and response, I see you, I hear you, I know you are there. I am aware of *you*—I see *you,* I hear *you,* I know *you* are there. That's almost so simple as to be ridiculous. But nothing has made more impression on me than just that very thing.

I went to a big church convention one time, and it was just as I knew it was going to be. You know, here's this thingy on you, and you meet somebody and he looks at your badge and says, "Hi—how are you?" Then before you can answer, he's looking over your shoulder for somebody better than you to talk to. And so you spend a week bumping into people,

Love says I'll put the paper down, I'll turn the knob off, I will look and I will listen, and all of me is present here to listen and to look at you.

never having time to talk to anybody and nobody ever really looks at you. "Oh, hi, how are you?" and you're on your way. *I don't know who everybody was looking for, but everybody was more important than I was.* And then sure as the world, some guy you don't especially want to see will just glue in on you. But love says I see you. Just like that—*see you.*

Here's a little thing—do you want a handle for all this? Love says look at the people you're talking to. Just look at them—go ahead, look at them. Don't look up there at the ceiling, don't look over there, don't put your hands in your pockets or draw on the ground. Don't kick the tire—just look at them. I see you.

I remember not too long ago—not long enough ago—I was sitting in the living room reading, and my daughter Susan said, "Daddy, Daddy—Daddy." And Mary Jo, her mother, said, "Why don't you, just for fun, count up the times you have to say 'Daddy' before he answers?" Now I heard that, and it didn't bless me a whole lot. I think the thing that hurt the most was that I'm not that kind of person. You know—I'm the warm, friendly, caring, outgoing type. I tell people that everywhere I go. I'm that type of person. But here I was reading a book—*actually it testifies to my fantastic powers of concentration.* And if that day at school was a normal day at school, I had listened and talked and shared with five or six students. And I came home and was sitting in my living room reading a book, and my very own daughter, who is very precious to me, was saying to me, "Daddy, Daddy—Daddy." That's not too good, is it? Love says I'll put the paper down, I'll turn the knob off, I will look and I will listen, and all of me is present here to listen and to look at you.

When I go home after spending a weekend speaking at a retreat or something, if it has been a normal weekend at home—you know, I've been gone, I've been wined and dined, I've had some good fellowship, I've had some solitude—it's about time for the dishwasher to go out or the radiator hose to break or the car battery to go down or some other dumb thing. Or the favorite trick—the bank balance getting all fouled up.

You see, I go back home to my wife, and she has been father, mother, and mostly chauffeur, and life has gone around and around. And I come back all filled up with what I've been doing, and she's all filled up with what she's been doing, and since I'm the one who's talking about love, guess who ends up listening. Here's the way it ought to be. *I'm not testifying, just telling you how it ought to be.*

When I go home, she'll say to me, "How did it go?" And I ought to say, "Fantastic. I wish you had been there. How did your weekend go?" And then I need to just be quiet for half an hour or more and just listen. You see, her words can come into my ears while I'm looking around waiting to tell her about this and that. But I need to just lay my words aside and look and listen and bring all of my attention to her—as a person. Isn't that what love means? All of me is here—at attention to care and to will your good.

It is really interesting that half the people who come into my office—*well, more than that, but I hate to admit it*—begin our conversations by saying, "Now I know you don't have any answers for me," which helps my ego tremendously. But really what people need from me is not answers, but a real live person listening and caring. That's what love means. I see you, I hear you, I know you are there. Listen to your husband—look at him. Listen to your wife—look at her. Listen to your children—look at them. What if we really listened; what if we really looked; what if we really saw each other?

When I was a child, we lived way out in the

country, way out in the San Joaquin Valley in central
California. It was 15 miles to Delano where we went
to school and 25 miles another way to Porterville
where we went to church, and in the other direction
there wasn't anything but the foothills of the Sierra
Nevada. If you came to see us, you came to see us, because nobody ever was just passin' by. We lived so far
out in the country that when the Electrolux man
came, we had him stay for supper.

My father was a quiet man, but I can remember
when people would drive all the way from town just
to talk to him. And I can remember times when people would come out, and I could hear the feeling and
emotion but not always the words they were saying to
Dad, and my dad would be saying stuff like "Hmm.
Well, my, my. Well, isn't that a sight? Hmm. Yes sir."

Then after a while the fellow would say, "Well,
Mr. Welch, I sure do thank you for your help." And
he'd get in his car and ride 20 miles back home, and
my father had said, "Hmm, now isn't that a sight?" I'll
tell you something—20 miles is not too far to go to
talk to someone who will listen and care and look
and understand and hear, even if all he says is, "Well,
what do you know?" That's true, isn't it? I'm getting
guilty about how little I really listen.

Let's talk about another handle we can put on
love. Love says I release you and will not judge you. I'm
not sure that writing about this will help my guilt
any—this is a hard one. I wish I'd written about it
when my children were little. I could have released
them then when they were too dependent to be released. It's much harder now that they are getting inde-
pendent. But we don't own each other. I don't own my
children, I don't own my wife. Our ultimate ties are ties
of love that must be freely given. I am commanded to
love but not to own or control or dominate.

Every once in a while I need to engage in a little mental exercise that puts my family up on a large pedestal about six feet high. I walk around the pedestal and look them over, one by one, and say, "I love you, I release you. I am responsible to you and for you, but I do not own you. I will not force you to find your fulfillment in my fulfillment—but I'll let you go to be your own person and find your own fulfillment supported by my love and care." How easy to write about this exercise and how hard to do it.

It is a wonderful experience to be with college students—to be about the age of their parents and not be a parent, to be a father figure to some of them and not be a father. *Though I'm not really a father figure because I'm too young.* I love them and care very much about them, but I do not own them and cannot control what they do or act as judge over what they do. I have no alternative—I must release them. And the marvelous, happy, surprising thing is this: Persons change in the atmosphere of releasing, unjudging love! I don't mean that it's a refined, Christian way of getting people to do what you want them to—but caring, releasing, unjudging love deliberately given in the love of Jesus becomes the agent for beautiful change in a person's life.

But, oh, the spirit of judgment. Do you know how to be happy with a group of people for a long time? Don't judge. A spirit of judgment will kill the honeymoon. That's precisely the point that brings about the old proverb: If you can keep the young converts away from the old saints long enough to get established, you'll be all right, because the old saints have been touched with a spirit of cynicism and judgment. Someone new comes into the church and says, "Isn't the pastor marvelous?" and "Isn't the choir fantastic?" and I can just hear the old saint: "Dearie, you just wait around awhile—

you'll see." That's true, isn't it? It's not right, but it's true. To the newcomer it's just heaven on earth in the community, but let them hang around awhile, and our cynicism will get them. It's catching, isn't it? It's the plague.

You would not believe some of the letters that students show me from their parents. And parents wouldn't believe that students show them to me either. I read letters that say in all kinds of ways, "I don't trust you . . . you aren't good . . . when will you ever change . . . you are always late . . . why don't you write . . . you aren't responsible . . . you are a disappointment . . . after all we've done for you . . . you'll have to get married . . . you'll get pregnant." I have seen the long arm of parental control and judgment reach across the miles from home to dormitory and almost destroy the precious, growing, seeking life of a young college student. *If I were speaking in public, I think I would be yelling about now.*

That deadly spirit of judgment is indeed the plague. But love, Jesus' kind of love, has the releasing, affirming power to stay the plague and heal our lives. What a handle—I love you, I release you, I will not judge you. We really do need each other. All this talk about love is not something ethereal and distant. It has handles that reach right down to where we are.

~2~

When You Run Out of Fantastic ...Persevere

Dean Nelson

"You never really move a college," Reuben said. "You blow it up."

That's how it felt for the chaplain who was used to speaking about the Christian community of faith and confession in the Pasadena auditorium that he helped build. That chapel was housed intimately on 17 acres where faculty members lived within walking distance of classrooms and offices. A lawn in the middle of the campus was used as a gathering place for students and faculty. The San Gabriel Mountains were within walking distance. When faculty members went on Friday afternoon hikes up those hills, everything that was terrible with the world on the way up was fine on the way down.

The new site in San Diego was 90 sprawling acres with scattered buildings, and it was in an upper-class neighborhood that was too pricey for most of the faculty members. Many, including Reuben and Mary Jo, ended up living a considerable driving distance from campus. And instead of speaking to an intimate gathering, Reuben now spoke from a makeshift platform in the middle of a gymnasium surrounded by students in bleachers along the walls.

"This was not a happy time for me," he said.

He had difficulty blindly accepting the statement of some that it was God's will for the college to move. His concern had less to do with the college itself, though, than with how in general Christians tend to apply a God's Will sticker to the bumper of a decision they have already made.

"Was it in fact the will of God that we move to San Diego?" he asked. "That couldn't be decided while we were still in Pasadena. It depended on what we did once we got to San Diego.

"I picture God as saying, 'You guys are moving, aren't you? Well, I'll go with you and help make something out of the shrapnel.'

"I suspect that's how it really is with most decisions we make," he said. "If we responsibly obey to fulfill God's vision in how to live, then we can say God led us here. If we do right, it can be OK."

This explodes the idea that God's will is a straight line to pursue—something in front of us. There Reuben goes again, letting God out of the box we've created. It's why people so emphatically love him. He stimulates thoughts that are outside of their traditional views on things.

"San Diego can't define our future or fulfill a will," he said. "Our response to God defines that.

"The Old Testament shows us that Moses took God seriously, and vice versa," Reuben said. "There was give-and-take with Abraham and Jonah, and others too. Instead of talking about God telling us what to do, I think God says, 'You choose, and I'll bless it.' Behind that is a personal, loving Presence."

Despite that knowledge, Reuben saw that things weren't as they should be. But the problem was more than just the college's moving and disrupting what they considered to be "home." Other things weighed on him.

Reuben's father was dying in a nursing home. His nephew, Bobby Poole, was dying of muscular dystrophy. The college president, Shelburne Brown, was dying of cancer.

Things were terrible. And the church, it seemed, was dying from either a lack of interest or from *too much* interest.

"It was during that period in the '70s where people wanted something wonderful to be going on in their lives and their churches. And if something exciting wasn't happening, then there must be something wrong," Reuben said.

Later, he wrote, it was a time when people wanted "continual emotional excitement. The sensualism of our age has affected our spiritual sensitivities. We hunger for the feeling of joy, the feeling of peace, and the feeling of the presence of God.

"In short, we want a life in Christ that is fantastic! Fantastic relationships, fantastic experiences, fantastic spiritual life—that's what we want, and we want it now!"

Consistent with this, the students in their enthusiasm could not accept that their college president was going to die, so they formed prayer chains for his healing and asked Reuben to participate.

"I tried to get into it, but I couldn't; and I couldn't tell them why," he said. "I was still grieving over the college move, and, more importantly, I had a handicapped daughter who was prayed over many times, and nothing happened with her."

He paused before he said what he was thinking. He was about to utter one of those statements that rattles the dentures of the comfortable. Then I realized he wasn't pausing for dramatic effect. He paused because his eyes had filled with tears.

"Prayer doesn't pull the ropes that ring the bells on the other side,"

> *"After people would testify in church, I wondered why I didn't have the same enthusiasm. I wasn't feeling very fantastic."*

he said. Out comes the handkerchief. He knows. No ropes or bells pulled Pamela out of an institution.

But the bigger issue during this period in his life was that he began to wonder about himself.

"I wondered what was wrong with me—why I wasn't OK," he said. "After people would testify in church, I wondered why I didn't have the same enthusiasm. I wasn't feeling very fantastic."

And, as one who has heard him preach countless times, I want to add a Reubenism right here and ask, *Is there anyone here who doesn't understand what he's saying? Anyone want to testify? Or is everyone fantastic except for Reuben? And me?*

God reached out to him through the Book of Hebrews. Not an easy book to understand, but the antidote for a culture that was very nearly worshiping their feelings about God rather than God.

Hebrews, Reuben discovered, speaks directly to believers who are on a journey, full of the burdens of everyday reality. It was written to people who had lost the joy of the faith.

"Ours is not the journey of a day, but of a lifetime; and *the issues are forever,*" he told the students as he began speaking out of this book. "The joys are real and there are times of excitement, but no feeling is permanent, and the whole range of emotions is experienced at some time or other along the journey."

Unlike the messages that became *We Really Do Need Each Other,* the messages he wrote out of Hebrews did not have years of contemplation and refinement. They came out of desperation.

"I didn't prepare these in my study or in the library, days or weeks in advance," he said. "These were written one hour before chapel, in the school archives room or anywhere else where I could get some quiet. I was just a little ahead of the posse."

Remarkably, during those desperate times of trying to write meaningfully out of a sometimes abstract book, Reuben found stability. He saw the message of Hebrews being Christ coming into our burdens, sharing our suffering with us, always obedient to the Father, wading through the deep waters to come to us and sometimes carry us.

"I didn't know this ahead of time, but I really needed to be carried then," he said, wiping his eyes. "And that's what happened."

But something else happened. That one hour before chapel became intense and productive.

"Those years of great trauma were the most productive of my life," he said. "Weird how that works."

By "productive" he doesn't just mean the sheer volume of work produced. He also means the way his messages were received.

"There was a real connection with the students when I preached this," he said. "We were in a transition, and I felt that I needed to speak to it."

It helped that, when he preached, the inner Voice in him agreed with what he was saying.

"I would preach these messages about the journey, about endurance, about being more than our feelings, about the long haul, about persevering, and the Voice in me kept saying 'Yes. Yes,'" he said. "Which is considerably better than the Voice saying, 'You don't believe this.' That severely limits your ability to speak effectively."

There was another emotion at work during those messages, though.

"I preached most of them when I was mad," he said. "I would say, 'I may be the only one, but I really care about this. We have too much sickness around us. What's wrong with us?'"

The Book of Hebrews became a similar call to a phrase he arrived at when he was studying Ephesians. Now Reuben has made it famous: *When nothing's happening, something's happening, because in the waiting God is working.* His more recent study in the Book of Genesis has developed the phrase further.

"The first thing God sanctified was not a place or a person, but a day," Reuben said. "The Sabbath. It established the rhythm of the week. It means God takes time seriously."

As any writer or reader can attest, most good stories have a beginning, middle, and end. At creation, Day One came before Day Five.

"God has ordained the time it takes to become His holy and mature people," Reuben said.

Then he *really* gets profound.

"Do you know that it takes the sovereign Almighty God about two years and nine months to create a two-year-old child?" he asks. "If you can't wait, I have a suggestion: Bring a newborn baby to the altar, anoint him with olive oil from the Holy Land, lay hands on him, and pray.

"If you pray and not grow faint, and hold on, in 24 months, boom! You'll have a miracle. I think that's the way God set it up."

Based on the Genesis account of how God views time and how Paul describes God's timing in Ephesians, Reuben now concludes that when things weren't feeling too fantastic during the transition from Pasadena to San Diego, God was working anyway. When nothing was happening, something was happening.

"I'm beginning to believe that the middle of the story is part of the God-ordained process too," he said, "which does not have predictable stages of steady growth."

God is at work, then, during the in-between—when a college, for instance, doesn't feel like the community it used to be. But it is healing, as are the participants.

A broken bone doesn't always feel that it's healing after it has been realigned. How long does it take to heal a broken leg? The miracle of God's healing has it at around six to eight weeks.

How long does it take to heal a broken heart?

"I don't know yet," Reuben says. "A long time."

It takes time to recover from the loss of a loved one—or a divorce or the loss of a home or job or reputation or virtue or integrity. Or a move from what used to be home.

"What if God is as much at work in the process of healing as He is in the healed-upness?" he asks. "What if God has ordained that it takes a while? What if, in the waiting, God is working?

"What if, when nothing's happening, something's happening?"

Something did happen as Reuben faced the loss of the college community he knew and the potential loss of a college president. He found that the Book of Hebrews breathed a consistent message: Jesus is Lord. What happens if the president dies? The breath of God replies, "Jesus is Lord."

"To say that Jesus is Lord means that He has entered into our suffering—not removed it," he said. So Jesus is less of an answer than He is a Presence—a sufficient Presence regardless of what we face. This is not about the circumstances life throws at us.

Looking to Jesus as Presence for the journey takes the focus off each day's events, and it takes the focus off each other. This does not diminish the premise of *We Really Do Need Each Other.* But it does recognize the limitations of what we can do and be for each other.

Jesus comes to us from God, *all the way* into our world, to meet us where we are, to act from among us and on behalf of us, with God. He enters completely into our weakness, our failure, and our humanness.

> *Jesus comes to us from God,* **all the way** *into our world, to meet us where we are, to act from among us and on behalf of us, with God.*

"I need a priest who's all mine," Reuben said in one message, "who really understands me, who doesn't say, 'Well, I'll see you later. I'd love to stay and pray, but I have to go now,' who really can take *all that I am to God."*

Even when he felt as if nothing was happening.

The messages he gave on Hebrews were 20 minutes each. "You can't even write home and ask for money in 20 minutes," he said. "But in those times the Book of Hebrews powerfully called us back to Christ."

He told the students that they didn't need any more "experiences." If they had been saved 25 times before coming to college, then number 26 probably wouldn't do them much good. He told them that their call was to continue the journey, whether it was "fantastic" or not.

And he began to believe it.

That was more than 20 years ago. He still worries about the desire for fantastic experiences, especially in worship services. He still thinks services emphasize feelings and events more than they should. He knows he runs the risk of dividing worship services along generational lines, but as he considers contemporary worship, he feels there is both good news and bad news.

The bad news, he said, is that "each generation codifies and institutionalizes their perception of the gospel." That helps him when he considers the state of the present-day Church.

"They don't know the difference between performance and worship," he said. "It has terrible theology and music."

After thinking about his assessment, he said, "I'd probably be better off not saying things like that."

And the good news?

"It's been worse," he said.

The important thing to consider is that if all we know about Jesus and the gospel is what we experience now, there is chaos— or worse, a perception that nothing is happening. And one of the ways to get Jesus unhinged from our personal perceptions is to look at the Book of Hebrews.

"No one generation understands the whole gospel," Reuben said. "Hebrews crosses all generational lines."

In all generations it shows that when it looks as if nothing is happening, something is happening. It might not all be fantastic, but it will have the Presence.

During the time of these messages, Reuben's father died. So did his nephew Bobby Poole. So did the college president, Shelburne Brown. And the students had an idea.

They transcribed the messages, contacted a publisher, and made a proposal: Proceeds of the book's sales could go to the creation of a new learning center on campus. Reuben and publisher agreed.

And something happened.

Reuben Welch

God Has Spoken

I don't know what you think about God or what your attitude is toward Him, but I wonder if you know and believe that He speaks and makes himself known. I think people come to God for many reasons and have many ways of expressing the quality of their relationship. But I think for me the richest thing about the gospel, at the practical life-level, is expressed in the words "fellowship" and "communication." To be able to pray, to be aware of God's presence, to know and believe He communicates with us—these are the most precious things in the world to me. I can't think of anything worse in the whole universe than out of the depths of my humanness and individuality, out of the cosmic loneliness of my soul, to cry out and have no answer back.

I heard about a dial-a-prayer for atheists—no one answers.... Now we laugh because it's easier to laugh than it is to cry. But that's the most awful thing I can think of in this whole world. But what Hebrews tells us, oh, what the whole Bible tells us, is that God SPEAKS. GOD has spoken!

Well, what does He say? JESUS! That's what God says. I don't know very much about God as Trinity. I love to think about it and talk about it and preach about it. I don't know very much about it, but a helpful idea to me is that the eternal Father expresses himself by the breath of His Spirit as He breathes the Word that is the extension of himself. And that Word that He speaks is JESUS. That Word becomes flesh and walks among us, and so we have in our history not just the propositional Word of God but also the personal, lived-out Word of God, breathed by the Spirit, spoken by the Father, expressing fully His nature and purpose.

God has spoken in His Son! That helps me! It helps answer the question, "What is God like?" GOD is like JESUS. That's what He is like. Because He has spoken *His* Word, we know what God is like! We have all heard it, and I have preached it often, that God is like Jesus. I wonder if we know how really fundamental this understanding is to all our Christian thinking.

Christian-type folks don't have the problem of God's existence. But we do have a problem—it is the problem of His nature. The question for us is not "Does God exist?" It is "What is God like?" How we respond to that question is fundamental to our response to every other issue of the Christian faith. Our believing, our loving, our trusting, our obeying, our surrendering, and our yielding are all conditioned by our perception of God.

I read somewhere that a false *mental* image of God is as dangerous as a false *metal* image of God. I believe that. What is your mental image of God? Can you believe that God has spoken in Jesus and in Him has communicated to us what He is really like? Can you let go old false ideas and jettison old erroneous mental pictures of God? When you say "God," think "Jesus," *God's personal, lived-out Word.*

That personal Word also tells us something about our world. All through the Bible we are told that God created the world through the Son and that the Son of God is the active Agent in creation, variously described as Word, or Wisdom, or Logos.

I don't know what that says about the inner nature of the triune God, but I know something of what it says about the character of the creation: that this universe is created by *the God who has revealed himself* in JESUS.

Celebration in Sorrow

I'm thinking of Bobby Poole, whose living presence 24 hours a day was a symbol of the reality of human suffering—an expression of the reality of human woe and tragedy and sickness and sorrow. And finally, he died.

And I don't care how much beautiful poetry you read or how much beautiful organ music is in the background; nothing takes that away—that stark reality of death and separation.

I think of some of the burdens that you carry—broken homes, broken hopes, broken dreams, and broken relationships. And yet *in the midst* of tragedy —even death—Christians can have a celebration. How can it be?

For one thing, because our Lord **has suffered and been tempted, he is able to help those who are [likewise] tempted** (Heb. 2:18). Christians are able to celebrate because they have the comfort and presence of the healing Holy Spirit right *in the midst* of their sorrow and *in* their tragedy.

Do you know what we need in our sorrow? We need some comfort! We need someone who can weave together the frazzled edges of our nerves. We need someone who can pour the balm of Gilead into the wounds that tear us apart.

Have you noticed that when we are at a funeral where people that we love are sorrowing, do you know what we do? We hug them. Sometimes we hug them as if we could burst their ribs! Why is this? I think it's an instinctive desire to break down the barriers, to get inside and to help heal, and to help lift.

You just wish you could get in there and just live in there and help. About the best you can do is just hug them tight or crush their knuckles in a handshake or say: "I love you." "I'm praying for you." "I care."

But isn't it wonderful that the presence of the Holy Spirit, unbound by the physical forces of the world, is able to minister to us deep in the stream of our inner consciousness. Deep inside where the wounds are, *He is present.* Hallelujah!

The values of a relationship: are they lost when a relationship is gone—when it's all over? After all the years, is there only to be said, "Well, it's all over now"?

Paul said in Corinthians, **Blessed be the God and Father of our Lord Jesus Christ, the Father of mercies and God of all comfort, who comforts us in ALL our affliction, so that we may be able to comfort those who are in any affliction, with the comfort with which we ourselves are comforted by God** (2 Cor. 1:3-4, emphasis added).

And I tell you it's a precious thing to know that God's healing presence can be with us! There's another reason why we are able to rejoice in the midst of sorrow and burden and death. It's because the values of our broken relationships are never ever lost.

Did you know God is the Conserver of values? You'll just have to forgive me for still being emotionally involved about my nephew's death, but that boy was a 24-hour-a-day care for years. And in a situation like that, there's a mighty lot of patience. There's a lot of just plain heroism. There's a lot of just plain old endurance. There's a lot of plain old self-sacrifice. There are times when you need sleep—but you can't sleep, and your nerves are frazzled but you have to be kind, and you want to do something else—but you back up and say, "Oh, well, some other time." When you stack all that up, there's a lot of value there! The times you've endured. The times you've been kind. The times you've prayed. The times that you said, "I'm sorry. Please forgive me."

The values of a relationship: are they lost when a relationship is gone—when it's all over? After all the years, is there only to be said, "Well, it's all over now"? NO! That's not enough! *God is the Conserver of values!* I just believe that with all my heart!

Does it matter if in the dead of night you are nice—instead of nasty? Does it matter if in the midst of temptations—you try? Does it matter if when you do something wrong—you say to somebody, "I'm sorry"? Is there any way to conserve the values that accrue in any kind of relationship?

Some of you have broken up with people; some very serious relationships have been severed. One of the hardest things about the whole business is that when you say good-bye, you feel as if all that's happened is lost. *But it isn't lost!* It's in the hands of one who is the Conserver of values, and it isn't lost!

Somewhere in the Book of Revelation there's a little phrase that I just love. I don't know all that it means, but it's saying a lot to me. It's about all the prayers of the saints being preserved like incense (5:8; 8:3-4). Now that's quite a symbol. Great golden bowls that hold the prayers of the saints! All the prayers that were ever prayed! All the struggles that were ever struggled, all the endurance that was ever endured, all the kindness that was ever kinded, all the help that was ever helped, all the love that was ever loved. All of that is preserved! And its value is secure in the keeping of God, *who is the Ground of our world and the Ground and Preserver of our values!*

So, when we wonder: Does it matter if we care? Does it make any difference if we try? Does anybody care if we struggle? Oh, yes. A thousand times—yes! The values of our human life are not lost. Isn't that lifting to our spirits!

And finally, Christians are able to celebrate *in the midst* of their sorrows, because they have a HOPE. When you come right down to it, that word is the word that really expresses all that we are as Christians. We are saved by it. We live in it.

That's the word that really expresses *all that we are* and *all that we believe.* Our hope is based on the resurrection of Jesus Christ from the dead that certifies that the last word is never death. The last word is never darkness. The last word is never hopelessness. This is God's world, and *the last word is LIFE.*

God is able to preserve the values of human relationships and to preserve the values of our prayers, and our struggles, and our efforts, and all that it means to be true—even in the face of death. Because God has raised Jesus from the dead, we live in hope. The living God, who raised Jesus from the dead, is present with us in our scene, sharing our suffering. **He himself likewise partook of the same nature, that through death he might destroy him who has the power of death, that is, the devil, and deliver all those who through fear of death were subject to lifelong bondage** (Heb. 2:14-15). That's why we celebrate in the midst of our sorrows and tragedies.

Some of you know the bondage of sorrow and suffering and carry with you the reality of tragedy and know the meaning of death. I want the Holy Spirit to say to you today, and to me, that Jesus sets us free, by His comfort, *in* our sorrows, by His conservation of our values, by His living HOPE made REAL in our hearts by the presence of His Holy Spirit.

Look at Him

You know, Moses was a very special kind of person. He was called to bring a nation into existence, but he wasn't the center of that nation. He was called to establish a new religion, but it wasn't called after his own name. He gave them laws and spoke eternal words, but they were not his laws and words—they were God's laws, God's words. What a faithful servant!

No, Lord, remember Your covenant—don't start something new with me. He recognized his place as a servant. And do you remember that later when he went back up the mountain, he said, **The people have sinned a great sin; but Lord, if You won't forgive them, blot my name out of the book of life** (Exod. 32:13, 31-32, author's paraphrase).

That sounds like Paul saying, **For I could wish that I myself were accursed and cut off from Christ for the sake of my brethren** (Rom. 9:3). See there on your imagination's screen Moses with the people of God, people whose very life and existence depended upon his faithfulness to them. How faithful! How caring! Consider Moses!

Can you now put another screen across the room and begin to consider Jesus? I wish we could sing together the old spiritual,

> *See Him in a manger—Amen.*
> *See Him in the Temple—Amen.*
> *See Him at the Jordan—Amen, Amen.*

Moses, faithful as a servant. Jesus, faithful as a

Son. Consider Him as in obedience to His Father—He speaks, He heals, He touches lives, and He gathers the people together. He is saying, **I came not to do my own will, but to do the will of my Father. . . . The words that I speak unto you I don't speak of myself, but of my Father, who dwells in me** (John 6:38; 14:10, author's paraphrases).

And Jesus **went about doing good** (Acts 10:38, KJV). Can you see Him? Can you see Him as He is faithful in Gethsemane? Can you see Him hanging there on a cross? Can you see by that mighty exodus that He accomplishes on the Cross—the new people of God gathered? Can you see Him risen in power and glory, at the right hand of God the Father? Can you see the outpouring of the Spirit, testifying that Jesus is Lord? Can you see Him in the midst of the congregation of the people of God, of every tribe and nation, and every tongue, and that congregation symbolized by the pilgrim people in the wilderness making their way to the land of Canaan?

And it includes all the nations, all the peoples, all across the centuries, all across this whole world. There is Jesus, with all His people. Can you see how their destiny depends on His faithfulness? And thank God He is faithful! Amen.

The writer to the Hebrews says, **Think about that! Set your mind on that!** (3:1, author's paraphrase). Jesus is faithful! He will not forsake. He will not forget. He will not give up. He is obedient. He is faithful to His task. He is faithful to His Father. He is faithful to us. Amen! Do you believe that?

You may give up on the Lord, but He will never give up on you. Now what all this has been saying to me is this: Don't give up your confidence in the hope we have in Jesus. When people first come by faith into newness of life in Jesus, they can trust Him for everything and have no doubt that God is in control and everything will turn out all right—in the long run. But sometimes as we go along and see the reality of our humanness and weakness and our times of failure, we begin to lose our confidence and our hope, and we become depressed and feel hopeless.

Am I talking to anyone who really feels hopeless? Once you had hope, but now you wonder if anything will really ever come of it. Do you know what this marvelous passage says? DON'T QUIT! Hang on! Keep the faith!

The writer is not saying: "Stir up confidence in yourself and try harder." You know what he says— **Don't let go of your confidence and hope. Consider Jesus. He is faithful.** *Look at Him* (3:6, 1-2, author's paraphrase).

In the midst of suffering, in the midst of temptation, in the midst of the hassles and the pressures and tensions that we face day by day, look to Jesus; He is faithful. Even as Moses was faithful as a servant, so Jesus is faithful as a Son. Faithful over the whole house, and we're in the house—we're part of the house, if we don't quit.... And the faithful Captain of our salvation will see us through! I really believe that!

I have a very dear friend who is today a wonderful man of God. I first met him many years ago, after he had been in the service, where he had lived a pretty rough life. One day, out in the woods by himself, he gave his life to Jesus. Then, as you might or might not understand, his troubles began. Before that, when he wanted to do something, he did it. But a new loyalty entered into his life. And he began the struggle of becoming a holy person.

For better or for worse, over a period of many years, I was to him a kind of father-confessor. And do you know, from a human point of view, there is no reason under the sun why that guy should be a Christian today. You want to talk about failure . . . you can't believe the failure. You want to talk about stress, about temptation, about struggle as he sought by the power and grace of God to rebuild the nerve grooves and rechannel his impulses and his desires and bring them into harmony with the love and the character of Christ? I'm telling you, he knew what struggle was— and what temptation was. And from any human point of view there was no reason why he should be a Christian today. But he just would not quit. He just would not give up.

I have this vivid mental image: when that brother dies and gets to heaven, the Lord's going to smile and say to him, "Well, you just *would* come . . . wouldn't you! All right, go on in." He may stumble all the way there, but he just *will* get there.

You know what our word so often is for the Christian life? FANTASTIC! Isn't that right? Praise the Lord for the young . . . FANTASTIC. Everything is *fantastic!* And as I read Hebrews, and read Hebrews, and read Hebrews, these words keep coming to me: *ENDURE! HANG IN THERE! DON'T QUIT! PERSEVERE!*

That's right. WHEN YOU RUN OUT OF "FANTASTIC"—PERSEVERE!

We are a pilgrim people following in obedience to the "rest" that is promised but not fully possessed here on earth. In the midst, right where we are now, let us consider Jesus, who was faithful. Faithful in obedience. Faithful unto death. He didn't give up and won't ever give up on you. Consider JESUS, **the author and [the] finisher of our faith** (12:2, KJV). He's the Head of this outfit. Praise God. And we're in . . . if we don't quit, if we hang in there!

Mental Images

When I think of Christ, there are a number of terms, concepts, and images that come to mind and are meaningful in my life. For instance, "Jesus is Lord."

Now the idea of Jesus as Lord is very meaningful to me. It computes. I understand it. It becomes a part of daily life. I think of Him as Savior, as Friend. Like in the song,

O worship the King ...
Our Maker, Defender, Redeemer, and Friend!
—Robert Grant

These are meaningful and practical mental images. But I think I must say to you that although the concept of Christ as Priest is an accepted concept, with me it has not been particularly significant in my life. Do you know what I mean by that? I don't know if that's true of you or not. If I were listing all the characteristics of Christ, I'd put "High Priest" in the list, but I wouldn't think about it very seriously. What has been happening to me as I've been working through the Epistle to the Hebrews is that I really am beginning to believe that Jesus really is a High Priest.

I think there are several reasons why the idea of Jesus as Priest does not really compute with us too well. One reason is that we associate priests with pagan religions. The mental image that comes to my mind is the South Sea island scene—you know, with the volcanoes in the background and the people singing "Ka-lou-ou-ahh," with the ukuleles going strum, strum, strum, strum. And the high priest gathers everybody around, for there's a drought in the land. They choose this beautiful maiden and lay her upon the altar, and the high priest drives the dagger in; of course, the camera fades for that scene.

We have weird images about priests. Sometimes,

when we think of priests, we think about the Old Testament with its picture of law and ritual—and there's blood, and gore, and awe, and smoke, and fire. Then the priest goes into the Tabernacle or Temple and does his thing.

It is clear that "priest" does not necessarily conjure up friendly images in us. As you know, Catholics have priests, pagans have priests, Old Testament people had priests—but not us good "Protestant" types! And I've been thinking about all this, and I've come to the conclusion that, in spite of our confused concepts of priesthood, we really do need one. We really do! And thank God we have one!

Let's talk about that some more. What do we mean when we say that Jesus is our Priest? The Lord has been helping me increasingly to see it in this way: Jesus, as Priest, comes to us from God, ALL the way into our world, to meet us where we are, to act from among us and in behalf of us, with God. Now the Book of Hebrews is saying to us that Jesus is capable of this—precisely because of His intimate relationship both with God and with us. The Priest is the Middleman, *der Mittler* in German. (Aren't you impressed?) Mediator—the One in the middle. One who is both God and man, human and divine.

When you come right down to it, we cannot handle our own relationship with God by ourselves.

You know, when you come right down to it, we cannot handle our own relationship with God by ourselves. You see, we do not have the holiness to come into His presence. We do not have the ability to eradicate the past. And from this point on, even if we could live good lives, there would be no way to go back and retroactively gather up enough merit to atone for the past. But there is One who has come among us from God himself, who does this thing for us. What we have in this passage is a magnificent view of both the divinity and the humanity of Christ. The Son of God has descended from the heavens—ALL the way from the throne of God.

And yet, on the other hand, look what this writer says about the humanity of Jesus. We are reading stuff we have heard and heard and don't even believe! Listen to this: **For we have not a high priest who is unable to sympathize with [us in] our weaknesses, but one who in every respect has been tempted as we are, yet without sin[ning]** (Heb. 4:15). And farther down: **During the days of Jesus' life on earth, he offered up prayers and petitions with loud cries and tears to the one who could save him from death, and he was heard because of his reverent submission. Although he was a son, he learned obedience from what he suffered** (5:7-8).

The whole thrust of the passage is this: the divine Son of God has come utterly into our world and taken to himself the realities of our total human situation. He understands all that our weakness means. He is able to understand us and do what we cannot do. We cannot make it without God. We need someone to take our case to Him. Someone who totally understands us, who is able to bear with us—to savvy our situation, to empathize with the reality of our needs. And Jesus is right there—right there!

I have a friend who's really sick both in body and spirit. And she hates herself, and nobody loves her, and everybody tries to but she won't really accept it but keeps rejecting it, and she cannot handle herself, cannot cope, cannot hang in there. And I've been thinking about her. The other day when I wrote to her, I said, "You really do need a priest—someone who understands you, who *really knows* and *really feels* where you are . . . and where you are coming from." You see, I can't do that. I can in part, but not *all* the way. And none of us can.

Do you know that there's a sense in which none of us can truly empathize with another? We have our own experiences, our own limitations, and are programmed in our own little ways. We can empathize partly—but not totally. And sometimes I say, "Well, God bless you. I'll be praying for you . . . good-bye."

But what my friend really needs is a priest who is all hers—who really understands and is able to take her case to God in ways that she cannot. And the glory of the gospel is that in Jesus, God is not out there waiting to be "come to," but in Jesus, God has come! And so the middle person is not just a human priest —He is God himself among us. And for us to give our case to Him is in fact to give it to God who really has the empathy, the understanding, the care, the redemptive power.

You know, I've been thinking about that . . . I really do need a priest! I really do! I need a priest who's all mine. Who really understands me. Who doesn't say, "Well, I'll see you later. I'd love to stay and pray, but I have to go now." Who really can take *all that I am to God,* who really has status and clout and power— and life with God. And what I'm hearing in this beautiful passage of Scripture is that Jesus Christ is that very Person. And I think what the Holy Spirit is saying to me, and I hope to us all, is that Jesus is right where we are, with total understanding and love, and He has been appointed by His Father to be our Priest, *to represent our case before God.*

Some of you are behind and pressured and going through times of temptation and stress. Some of you have had times of tension or broken relationships. Some have experienced the tragedy of death, sorrow, and sickness. You know what we need? We need a priest. You know why we need a priest? Because of our weaknesses. The Priest takes our weaknesses to God. And God's the One who appoints Him. He knows what we need. Jesus is our High Priest. Praise His name!

Grow Up

We float along the surface of life, unfulfilled and empty, not really thinking about things—not really seeking, growing, learning. The great tragedy is that our lethargy leads to a high degree of susceptibility to just about *any* teaching that comes along, or any movement that surfaces, or any emphasis that is the current fad. We really are vulnerable to that—especially if the leader of a group is highly articulate, and simplistic, and absolutistic, and has a little charisma. *We just go ye-a-h!* We really do, don't we!

Somebody comes onto the scene preaching health, wealth, and happiness through trusting God and sending money, and we just get on board like mad! We don't know whether it's true or not, so we are led astray or led aright. Either way is purely accidental. We're just children. Someone comes along with simple, absolute, authoritative answers that solve everything—six easy steps to do this, five ways to do that, and four laws to do this—and we just grab it like it's everything. We run here, and then we run there, and we're children—babes!

And I'm worried about myself too. What have we come to that's our own from the Word of God? It's something to even have your own doubts—you know that? It's bad when you've got secondhand doubts! Are we babes drinking from the nipple of whatever bottle is offered to us at the time? I think about that! And I really am hearing the call of God that we need to grow up. We really do need to grow up. . . . Well, what are we going to do?

I know this much for sure—the answer isn't to go back or to give up. . . . Verses 4 to 8 in Heb. 6 speak to us about not being able to restore again to repentance those who've had all these blessings but then turn and reject, and then turn their backs on God. There is nothing left for them but despair. I don't understand that. And I know for sure I don't like it.

But let me just say this much: I think we understand the difference between sin and apostasy, between failure and rejection of the gospel. It's one thing to fail; it's another thing to turn your back on Christ as God's Way of salvation and reject His offer of love. When you do that, brother, when it comes to that, sister, there's nothing else.

The writer doesn't say that anyone in fact has fallen into apostasy or fallen away. If anyone did, it would be an awful thing. But he goes on to say, thankfully, **[I am] persuaded [of] better things of you** (v. 9, KJV). And I take that for myself and for you too. Praise God!

I'm talking to some of you who have heard the gospel all your life, and you're playing around with attitudes and behaviors, with lifestyles and relationships that are terribly destructive. And somehow you feel that it really doesn't matter. You still are acting like babes, even when there are *ultimate issues involved.*

We know the facts of life and that we don't stay neutral for very long. And folks, to fall back, away from the best we know, is no way to go! There is only one way to go, and that's *on to maturity!*

I've been hearing that a long time. I know I'm old in years, but I'm dumb, and I'm young, and I feel like a baby. And the word of the Lord comes to me—"It's time to grow up some." And I wonder if the word of the Lord needs to come to you like that. We can't go back, so, children, let's go forward to maturity!

I don't know if I ought to talk about this or not, but I just think I will. You know, we have revivals and special evangelistic emphasis, and that's good. But I have to confess to you that I'm troubled and hassled by some of it. My guess is that most students who come to a Christian college have already committed themselves to the Lord 25 times or so. When you have been saved 25 times by the time you get to college, what do you need? Number 26? Fourteen verses of "Just As I Am"? Seventeen of "Almost Persuaded"? Nineteen of "Tell Mother I'll Be There"?

Do you know what I mean? I think that what we need to do is to quit starting over again and *start growing.* We need to grow up.

Well, we're getting near the end of this talk, and it's time for me to bring out the big magic word for growth. You ready? Everybody listen. I've found a beautiful, fantastic, magic formula for how to grow. Praise the Lord! I've been waiting for it all my life, and now I've finally found it—and I'm here to share it.

You know what I find in this Book of Hebrews? Do you know what the magic formula is? Don't quit! Trust God. Be patient. Hang in there!

You know, that's terrible—after laying it on us that we're a bunch of babies and we need to grow up! Here comes the great climax and the great magic truth—hear it, everybody—"Believe God." "Trust the promises." "Be patient."

Just like that! It isn't magic after all. And it isn't something for a few special souls who have unusual strength. It is a common, doable truth for us all. Don't quit! And men like Abraham and the Patriarchs, Moses and the Prophets, Jesus and the Apostles, and all the saints through all the ages, have become mature in God—holy men of God—because they *believed,* and they were *patient,* and they *endured,* and they *trusted,* and they *obeyed,* and they *didn't quit.* They hung in there, and they grew, and they grew, and they grew!

So, children, I guess when it comes right down to it, we grow up by believing and by hanging in there —by not quitting, by trusting in the care of our High Priest.

Losing Weight

That word "race," it seems to me, is both good and bad. I think the imagery is good in the sense that it means that life is dynamic and not static. It means that we're going somewhere—and we aren't stationary.

There is a contest going on. There is life, there is growth, and good things are happening. *There is a struggle to be struggled. There is endurance to be endured. There is a goal to be achieved*—and we aren't just circling around. I wonder if we know that.

The whole imagery tells us that our journey is for real. And the call to us is to **lay aside . . . weight, and sin which clings so closely, and . . . *run with perseverance* the race that is set before us** (Heb. 12:1, emphasis added).

Now the imagery of the race is bad if it conjures up the idea that we have to struggle, struggle, struggle, and if we get tired and fall down, then everybody else will pass us up. If it conveys the idea of competition—always panting and laboring, then it is a bad image. But if we remember that we're on a journey and that we don't stand still, either going forward or slid-

ing back, then the image is correct. We don't experience a brief time of struggle and growth followed by
a lengthy plateau—level and smooth—on which we
"glide along" toward God. If we drift very long, we
start settling back. So we need the imagery of a race
to tell us that life is dynamic—and that it is moving. It
has a goal and it demands endurance from us.

Now this race is in fact **set before us.** There are
some serious implications in that phrase. It seems to
carry with it the idea that the race is our providential
appointment. Just as the goal is set before us to be enjoyed, the race is with us to be run.

That helps me! The race is given to us. Just as
much as our Lord Jesus looked to the goal that was
set before Him, enduring the Cross, despising the
shame, so we, too, who look toward the goal realize
that the race is the course ordained for us in the
achievement of the goal. And that means that a part
of what the Christian life is all about is hanging on in
the struggle. But we don't want to struggle.

A lot of us have a tendency to fall into an "if only" syndrome. You know—if only my house were different, I could be more holy. If only students wouldn't
knock on my door, I could read the Bible more. If only
my phone wouldn't ring, I could be far more religious. (That's fact, folks!) If I didn't have to hassle, hassle, hassle—didn't have to mow the lawn or pay the
bills. The more I think about it, the holier I could be
—if only, if only, if only.

That's what you're thinking, too—if you didn't
have so much homework, if you had a different room-
mate, if you had a different wife or husband, if you
had more money, if you had a better job, if you'd get
more sleep at night, if you didn't have so many temptations, if you weren't so weak, if you weren't so ugly.
The whole business—if, if, if, if.

Do you know what we need to see? We're in the world, right where God put us, and a part of the appointment of divine providence is the faithful running of the race. And the dominant verb in this whole passage is run—with perseverance the race that is set before us. Don't quit! Just persevere. Like the man said one time, "When you run out of fantastic—persevere!"

I wonder where we ever got the idea that if we really were all-out for God, we would be continually joyful, never blue or lonely, always praising God and on top of the mountain every day.

Our pendulums swing and our emotions go up and down, but what God wants to do is to develop a steadiness in us. I'm praying for that in myself. It doesn't bless me a whole lot that after more than 50 years I'm still struggling with it. But I am.

And I think sometimes we get the feeling that if we were really what God wanted us to be, we'd always be excited.

I wonder where we ever got the idea that if we really were all-out for God, we would be continually joyful, never blue or lonely, always praising God and on top of the mountain every day. I'm talking to some of you who think that's the truth. And I'm just going to stand right here and look you straight in the eye and tell you that such notions are not the truth! Just don't you believe it!

You see, the emotional dynamic of the Christian

life is not that much different from that of any other
natural life that comes from God. Our natural life
doesn't maintain a constant emotional equilibrium.
Neither does our spiritual life. Do we really understand that?

If we look at it in the context of "life as journey"
and in the context of the **race set before us,** we begin to see the Christian life as having varying phases
and differing moods. There is high emotion at the
starting blocks—at the beginning of the race. There is
high emotion that comes with the honeymoon. There
is high emotion that comes with the beginning of the
Christian life. There is great excitement when you
come up to the edge of the pool for the race. But
there's a difference between the emotion at the beginning of the race and how you feel when you've
swum a couple of laps.

You will find this hard to believe, but I ran the
"1320" years ago. And I know the difference in how
you feel at the beginning, and how you feel in the
middle, and how you feel at the end.

Would anyone guess where we are in our race?
You're right. We're somewhere in the middle. Between the "already" and the "not yet"—between the
excitement of the start and the thrill of the finish. And
do you know what the Word of God is? Persevere!
Hang in there! Don't quit!

It is really unrealistic to assume that if we really
are all that we ought to be, we will always be on a
spiritual honeymoon. It simply is not true! This attitude becomes the devil's own weapon against us!
Newness does not stay new. And so the word of the
Lord comes: **Run with perseverance the race that
is set before us** (Heb. 12:1).

Now in this context there are a couple of things
that the writer to the Hebrews says. Would you be im-

pressed if I tell you that there are a couple of participial phrases here? Listen to this: **Let us . . . lay aside every weight, and sin which clings so closely** (v. 1).

I want to talk about that verse for a minute. I hate to tell you this, but I found out that basically the meaning of this word **weight** is "bulk" or "mass." We're supposed to lay aside bulk, weight, or mass. When you come to the blocks to run the relays, you don't put your robe on—you take it off. When you come up to the edge of the pool for the race, you don't wrap towels around you—you take them off. And if you've been carrying weights in training, then when you come to the real thing, you let them drop. And that's what God is saying to us.

What is a weight? A weight is anything that hinders us on our journey. And I hear those words fill this building—and they're scary. The call of God to us is to run a race that is for real! Do we know that? The issues are ultimate! Our destiny is either life or death. And the call of God is to lay aside what causes us to stumble.

I've got a weird imagination and I have a clear mental image of this. Look with me. Here is the Christian pilgrim running up the pathway to glory. Can you see him? There he is . . . his spindly legs are pounding the turf. He is on his way. He looks like a wise man escapee from the Sunday School Christmas program. He has his robe. He has his sash. And he's running up the King's Highway. And pretty soon his robe begins to flap in the breeze, and his sash comes loose and it wraps around his legs—and he falls. Then he gets up, gathers up, puts on a Band-Aid, and starts running again, and the wind begins to catch his clothes and his sash begins to flail in the wind, and he trips and stumbles.

Are you catching on? I'm talking to some of you who are running the Christian race just like that! You start out for God, start out to do right, but the things you're wearing and have been carrying with you all these years trip you up and cause you to fall. Do you know what the word of God is? Take it off, put it aside.

I sure wish I had time to tell you all your weights. That would bless me! But my real problem is finding out what mine are. I don't know what yours are, but some of you are stumbling. I don't know what your weights are—but I've learned from this passage how to find out. I'll tell you how to find out what they are: start running! As long as you're standing around, you can be all wrapped up. You can have towels and weights and bathrobes and sashes. You can be bound hand and foot, and it won't make much difference. But if you start moving toward God, you will begin to find out what causes you to stumble. *And what causes you to stumble has got to be laid aside!* Amen!

I am not sure we are called to be, as someone put it, "streakers for Jesus," but I am sure that we are called to lay aside those sins that so easily beset and destroy and run with perseverance the race set before us—**looking unto Jesus the author and finisher of our faith** (Heb. 12:2, KJV)!

Look Away

I've been thinking about my grandfather, affectionately known as Uncle Buddy Robinson. He was a well-known and widely traveled evangelist in our church. Almost everywhere I go someone still remembers him, though he died more than 30 years ago. I must confess that when I have finished preaching all my "great stuff" to the congregation, I am "unblessed" when one of these old-timers shakes my hand and says: "I knew your grandfather." Sometimes I want to answer, "Is that all you've been thinking about while I've been yelling these great theological points at you?" I seldom have the courage to say those words!

Anyhow, I've been thinking about my grandfather. He was here. He ran his race. He finished. He did his thing. He had his time—and now he is gone. Me too, someday. But now I am living. I'm here. It is my time to do my thing and be obedient to God!

And, especially now, I am thinking about my father who died a few days ago. How can it be that he is gone? He is, thank God, part of that great company of witnesses. But he lived his life—had his time—and now is gone. Me too, someday.

And I wouldn't use all those first person singulars, except that each of us can say the same thing. It's true of you too. Some of you have grandfathers and great-grandfathers and parents and loved ones who were here, and now they aren't. But YOU ARE. It's your turn now. Others have come and passed on the heritage. They have offered, walked, obeyed, trusted, endured, were true and faithful—and they've gone on. And now we are here.

And do you know what the call to us is? I can hear it. **Let us [here and now] run with perseverance the race that is set before us** (Heb. 12:1). They ran the one that was set before them, and this is the one set before us. Here we are, and God says to run it with perseverance, **lay[ing] aside every weight** (v. 1).

Almost wished I hadn't preached on that. I'd love to run that one by again. I still hear the call to lay aside every weight **and [the] sin which clings so closely** (v. 1), and run with perseverance the race that is set before us.

The way to heaven is not the 30-yard dash. Some of us have assumed that's just what it is—maybe 100 yards at the most. So we're going to make a great burst of speed, and a 100-yard dash to heaven! And if we are lucky, even avoid the Tribulation!

Is that what we think? The Christian life is not a short dash; it's a long run. It really is! So we are called to persevere and endure. Now having laid aside the weights, we are to keep running—keeping our eyes fixed on Jesus. **Looking to Jesus the pioneer and perfecter of our faith, who for the joy that was set before him endured the cross, despising the shame, and is seated at the right hand of the throne of God** (v. 2).

What are we to do as we run our race? It isn't that we spend all our time looking for stuff to lay aside. The way you find out what your weights are, remember, is to start running, and what hinders you in the race needs to be laid aside. But the whole direction of the passage is not to the laying aside but toward persevering in the race. Having laid aside our weights, we are to keep looking to Jesus.

And I've been thinking about what it means to look to Jesus. To look to Jesus as we run the race means that we look away from everyone, and everything else, and fix our attention and the inward gaze of our lives *on Him alone!* I'm almost embarrassed to say that because we have heard it all our lives, haven't we? But about every testimony of backsliding we have ever heard has at its root, "I got my eyes off the Lord, and I got them on people . . . and people let me down."

Now I'm not trying to say we don't really need each other. Oh no! But we know that when we look to people, they may let us down. That's a fact, isn't it? Every place I've ever been there were folks who just disappointed me flat out. Do you understand that? People will let us down. And if we are going to endure, we have to have our eyes fixed on someone who won't let us down. People around us will sometimes disappoint us. But we've got to look away from other persons as our dependency, as our models, and look to JESUS as our Model. We are running our race, looking to Jesus—the Pioneer and Perfecter of faith, the Originator, the Consummator, the Trailblazer, the Author, the Finisher of our faith—not only the One in whom we believe, but the One who himself was faithful. We need to look away from everyone and everything else and get our dependency on HIM.

Do you know what I think? I think a lot of us are trying to find meaning for life, happiness for life, in the relationships we have with other people. Some do so with a boyfriend or girlfriend, others with a husband or wife, boss or coworker. I remember when Dr. Paul Culbertson (longtime professor of psychology at Pasadena-Point Loma College) was talking about the love songs of today that ascribe to the lover attributes that can only properly be ascribed to God.

Those terms belong only to GOD. We put too much of our dependence in human relationships and not enough on Jesus. Who we are and what we are— our joy, our meaning, are to be found only in Him! Other relationships will often disappoint us. But isn't it a wonderful truth, that though others have disappointed us, we ourselves have never been a disappointment to others? Praise the Lord! What a consolation! Nobody here but us "nondisappointer" types.

No! I think the hardest burdens we bear are often tied in with the fact that not only are we disap-

> *But isn't it a wonderful truth, that though others have disappointed us, we ourselves have never been a disappointment to others?*

pointed, but also we have ourselves plainly, clearly, disappointed others. Isn't that right! It doesn't bless me to say it, you know. I'm the caring, friendly, consistent type who loves people and cares. But sometimes, sometimes I don't come through. And you know what this passage from Hebrews says? We're to look away from ourselves and our faith, and our lack of faith, our abilities, and our disabilities, our strengths, and our weaknesses, and look only to Jesus.

And do you know what's really at the heart of this passage? That we are to look to Jesus as our *Example* of faith, and the example in Jesus that is placed before us is His endurance of the Cross. We are, then, to let His own attitude toward His cross, His endurance, and His faithfulness, be ours as well. Jesus lived and died by faith, and that makes Him the greatest in the whole long line of believing persons.

And from the time He moved out of His baptism experience into the temptation experience and into his public ministry, He said, **My meat is to do the will of him that sent me, and to finish his work** (John 4:34, KJV). And all through His life He lived by faith. He loved His Father, trusted in His Father, depended upon His Father, and in the hour of His death He surrendered himself to His Father. And do you know what we believe? That His Father raised Him from the dead and exalted Him at the right hand of the throne in glory, and now we are to look to Him and put our trust in Him and not in anything or in anyone else.

What God Wants

What is God's motive? What is the direction of the love motive that moves toward me in discipline? It is that I may be a partaker of His holiness. I wonder then: Is it true that there really is no authentic sharing of the character of God without suffering? Is there no way for us to become truly holy persons without discipline? The purpose of God in His dealings with us is to make us holy. That's right here in the Word, as clear as anything I've ever read.

And it seems to me that the expression of this is to be found in the peaceful fruits of righteousness. **For the moment all discipline seems painful rather than pleasant; later it yields the peaceful fruit of righteousness to those who have been trained by it** (Heb. 12:11). Friends, God wants to do something in us. God wants to do more in us and for us than we have yet experienced. God wants to make us holy persons.

I've noticed during these past few years of my life two things, simultaneously. First, there is a growing disenchantment in some quarters of the church with the old terms that have at other times been precious— words like "sanctification." Have you ever noticed that when the young (and the unyoung) talk about sanctification, or holiness, they always tag on a little phrase or two—"whatever that is" or "whatever that means." The term "sanctification" has lost a lot of its lure power. But do you know what's going right along with that? An increasing desire to be holy. There is a holiness that is produced by faith in Christ our Lord, who, **that he might sanctify the people with his own blood, suffered without the gate** (13:12, KJV).

There is an experience of God's sanctifying grace to cleanse the heart and set our wills in harmony with His. But when that inner oneness with and devotion toward God begin to work their way out into the channels and the avenues, the nerve grooves, the imagination patterns, the habit patterns, the lifestyles we have, we discover that it takes a bit of doing to develop a holy character. That's not the kind of thing you get at an altar or any other place of full surrender. But it is the kind of thing God wants to do in us through His working in our lives. And what I am feeling in myself, and what I'm praying for you, and discerning among you, is really a growing desire to be holy. We really do want to be holy, to be a godly people, a holy people.

That's what God wants us to be too. That's the ultimate purpose behind the disciplinings, in and through the sufferings, the troubles, and the hardships. That's precisely what God is seeking to develop in us. You know, we aren't told what the disciplines are, or what the sufferings are, what the chastisement is, even as we are not told what the weights are, or what the surrounding sin is. But we are told what God's purpose is for us in them all!

I know in the depths of my heart that the whole discipline process in our relationship to God is designed to strike at our pride and bring us to obedience—to make us submissive to His will, that we may grow in likeness to His character. And I have to say that I'm disturbed because in myself, and in all of us, it's so easy to have exciting experiences—we're long on emotion and short on character. We're high on emotion, and low on morality and perseverance. And there are among us the sins of the flesh. God wants to purge our fellowship of these sins that destroy and damn, wreck and doom. But God also wants to work on the sins of the spirit—self-centeredness, self-will, self-dependence, pride, our thought life, our attitudes, our habits, our ways of talking and thinking—He wants to make us godly people.

And I guess what's on my heart, when it comes right down to it, is this: sometimes trouble comes to us, and I don't understand all about it, but I know that a part of what we need to do is back off and pour it out to God, and *expose to God the depths of our lives* and say: "Lord, what are You trying to say to me? What changes need to take place in me?"

Oddly enough, I find myself saying sometimes to people who talk to me in times of relationship breakups, tension, and stress, "You know, sometimes a relationship needs to break up in order that the persons involved may grow to be truly persons and be their own people and not lean so hard on one another."

Sometimes I get the feeling that couples just glue onto each other like a couple of cantaloupe halves, you know, trying to make a whole. And the vacuum is what holds them together. And, as you know, that doesn't generally make too good a marriage. What you really need is two whole persons who express their own individuality and care for each other in responsible ways. Sometimes God moves into the flow of life and causes us to back off, because He wants us to become the kind of person that the kind of person we want, will want. And I talk about that because somehow it's tied into our relationship to God.

Well, I'm convinced of this, that God has something to say to us, that He is not uninvolved in all of these things that confront us, and that what He is saying to us, what He is confronting us with, is the call to share His holiness, which manifests itself in righteousness as its fruit. We need to take a different attitude toward our troubles. God *is at work in them, is present in them,* and what He is doing is conforming us to the image of His Son—to share in His holiness.

Two Mountains

Two great mountains—Sinai and Zion. On which one are you living? The writer to the Hebrews tells us that we are not come to Mount Sinai, to that which **burned with fire, nor unto blackness, and dark-**

**ness, . . . and the sound of a trumpet, and the
voice of words** or to the awesome fear that disquiets
and separates. Instead we are come to Mount Zion,
the city of our God in the mountain of His holiness;
**to an innumerable company of angels, to the
general assembly and church of the firstborn,
. . . and to God the Judge of all, and to the spirits
of just men made perfect, and to Jesus the mediator of the new covenant, and to the blood of
sprinkling, that speak[s] better things than that
of Abel** (12:18-19, 22-24, KJV).

Look, the whole Epistle has taught us that all
God's dealings with men are involved in two great
movements in history. One is the dispensation of
preparation and promise—of weakness and failure.
The other is one of fulfillment and perfection—of
eternal life. The Epistle has taught us, too, that though
we have our place in the new dispensation, yet like
the Hebrews, we may still be living, for all practical
purposes, under the old dispensation—really experiencing nothing of the better covenant; still living like
old Israel—in weakness and sin.

And so we understand Sinai as a symbol of law,
of fear, of dread. And as I say that, I wonder in my
heart how many of us are still finding ourselves thinking about God in terms of fear, in terms of dread—still
living in legalism and under law, still under the old
covenant. Under the old covenant, when one thinks
of God the mental image is not one of grace and love,
mercy and forgiveness—but darkness and tempest,
and wrath and anger.

I wonder about that! I wonder about whether
we have indeed opened our hearts to the new
covenant that God has made known for us in Jesus
our Savior. Sinai says, **Keep back, no admittance!**
But Zion says, **Come; for all things are now ready**

(Luke 14:17, KJV). The law says, **Your iniquities have separated between you and your God** (Isa. 59:2, KJV). The gospel says, **We are brought nigh** (see Eph. 2:13, KJV). Hallelujah! I love the "pilgrim" feel of the Epistle to the Hebrews. I suppose part of it is because it fits in with the idea that we are on a journey.

Well, let me ask you this day, "Where are you on your journey?" Do you know we have the privilege of being at Zion? And some of us are still living in Sinai—in fear, in legalism, in dread. Some of us are still trying to build our lives by ourselves, on ourselves, doing our own thing, finding our own security. But thank God we can have grace!

Well, do you need some? Anybody here need some grace? Why don't you take some? Take several! It's free! You don't deserve it, can't earn it, but it's provided, and it's here—now!

We Really Do Need to Listen

Dean Nelson

You know a book has made an impact when it still reveals insights a long time later. In the case of Henri Nouwen's book *Reaching Out,* the impact on Reuben has lasted almost 25 years. Published in 1975, the book explores the three dimensions of the spiritual life: reaching out to our innermost self—from loneliness to solitude; reaching out to our fellow human beings—from hostility to hospitality; and reaching out to our God—from illusion to prayer.

It is the section on "reaching out to our fellow human beings" that has particularly stuck with Reuben, because it resonates so well with how he witnessed the way his parents treated others. As he mentions in *We Really Do Need Each Other,* he was amazed at how people would drive many miles out of town to his family's citrus farm to talk to his father, and all his father would do was give one of the following replies:

"My, my."

"Isn't that a sight."

"Well sir."

And this helped countless people.

Reuben's father opened up space in his life and let people in. Years later Reuben read in *Reaching Out* that the way to reach out to others is to adopt a voluntary poverty of mind and heart that opens an empty space of hospitality so that we can receive the thoughts, feelings, and experiences of others. It describes a voluntary laying down of our fullness. And despite his years of teaching and being chaplain, he realized that, when students came into his office, they weren't always looking for his depth of understanding.

"They needed me to lay down my fullness, put aside my wisdom, swallow my insight, to open up an empty space for them," he said. "Not judge, interrupt, or finish their sentences." Just as his father did, in his "office" out on the citrus farm.

The implications of this kind of action reach pretty far. What if, he wonders, family members laid down their fullness before one another?

"We need to listen to our children without interrupting them," he said. "Then we need to revive them from fainting."

What would happen, he asks audiences, if husbands would listen to their wives and not interrupt? If they laid down what they were doing and looked at their wives while their helpmates spoke?

Then he quickly adds:

"Ladies and gentlemen, we have just entered Fantasyland."

And he's on a roll.

"Ladies, if your husband's words are sharp, maybe he's trying to get them in edgewise!"

But opening up space for one another means we make room for them. Funny how that connects with how we really do need each other. And it's funny how it mirrors the way God comes to us—opening up hospitable space for us.

"I think the word for it is 'grace,'" Reuben says.

God creates space for us to say our say, gripe our gripes, parade our arguments, lift up our praises, call out our fears, reveal our needs and sins and guilts.

"God opens up space and invites us in," Reuben says. "It is in that space that we can *become.*"

And one of the ways we become is by asking questions. Personal questions. Secret questions. Questions we might be embarrassed to admit we wonder about. Questions rooted in fear or doubt or insecurity or failure. In Reuben's understanding, God provides ample room for questions. He points to Jesus' farewell discussions with His disciples in John chapters 13—17 as evidence. Much of what we know about the nature of God comes from Jesus' responses to the disciples' questions. And, as further evidence of Jesus' opening space for us, Reuben points out that most of those questions came as interruptions to what He was trying to tell them in the Upper Room.

Questions like Where are You going? and How can we know the way? and What is God like? and How does Jesus become real to us? What does this relationship with Jesus mean in our daily lives? and Who is the Holy Spirit? and What is God's glory? and What does it mean to be holy? and What does it mean for us to be one with each other? and Whose side is God on? are all in those wonderful chapters, spoken by Jesus, responding to questions and interruptions.

Every gift, promise, commandment, warning, and resource is in those answers. And they came as a result of Jesus' creating open space, laying down His fullness, so the followers could become disciples—so they could know.

Reuben's interest in these chapters came from at least two levels—both extremely personal. Joe Mayfield, a colleague and friend at Pasadena College, loved the Gospel of John.

"I wanted to love the book, too, because I loved Joe," Reuben said.

But the other reason for exploring the chapters came out of confusion about the word "holy."

"I had tried very hard to find out what it meant to be holy," he said. "I wanted to be a holy person, and I sensed the same desire among the college students. But we were operating without the proper language for it. That language is in John 17."

Part of the confusion about the word was in how the church was using it to describe things.

"What do we mean when we say this is a 'Holiness college,' or a 'Holiness church'?" he asked. "There are 100 definitions for it when you attach it to an institution.

"We are instructed by Jesus to 'be holy.' For an institution, the more accurate position should be to say, 'We are a church seeking to be holy' rather than saying, 'We're a Holiness institution.'"

Reuben's study of these discussions took him from knowing what the words said to having his life directed by those very words.

So, exactly what does it mean to be holy? In John 17, Reuben summarizes Jesus' words with this: To be holy is to be different by virtue of belonging to God.

"The will of God is not a thing that comes on us," he says. *"It emerges and gives us our druthers. The will of God is to give us the desires of our hearts."*

It also means to be a participant in the purposes of God.

"We've all heard that God has a plan—a call—a will," Reuben says. But as soon as he utters the words, an astute listener will see that he or she is being set up for something big. Those terms are a problem, just as so many other terms have been to him (and us). Characteristically, he sees those words pointing us in different directions from how they are traditionally used.

"The will of God is not a thing that comes on us," he says. "It emerges and gives us our druthers. The will of God is to give us the desires of our hearts."

Just as he has taken careful aim at revival preachers who

mess up the audience with all of their certainty, he now has another group in his sights.

"People who say, 'I had a call to the mission field, but I fought it,' are living under a pretty strange construct of who God is and what His purpose is in the world," Reuben says. "I can't dispute that they think this, but for myself, I can't think that way.

"Why, if you are afraid of snakes, would God call you to the mission field somewhere in a jungle? God's will is congruent with His creation."

It disturbs people to hear him talk like this. But it would disturb him to talk like them.

"A pastor once asked me, 'What do we have to hold us steady?' and I said, 'I don't know.' He said, 'I do—it's my call.' I'm glad he feels the way he does. It isn't that clear to me."

Promises in general aren't a very good way to maintain any relationship. We make promises to our kids that we intend to keep, and then they come to us when we can't come through and say, "But you promised!" Relationships aren't sustained by promises. Reuben preaches about Peter making a promise to Jesus. He had good intentions. He believed that what he was saying was true. He would never deny Jesus. Would he?

Instead of promises, relationships are sustained with a continual, deliberate laying down of ourselves for one another. Participating in the shared purpose.

While Reuben can't identify with a will of God that is based on promises or conflict, what he *can* identify with is the will of God that is revealed throughout the Bible. God's cause in the world is to heal, unite, and reconcile His entire creation back into right relationship with Him. Our call from God is to participate in the healing, uniting, and reconciling. That's all we really need know about God's will, he says. He comes to these conclusions after studying the Book of Ephesians.

"Over the years we put together these amazing images of God and attributes about Him," Reuben says. "And then when you look at what He says about himself, those images look pretty dumb."

With that, he adds his own beatitude:

"Blessed are those who have it all figured out, for they shall be blissfully wrong."

Here is what the Bible says about our calling: it comes from one of Reuben's favorite passages, out of Eph. 4: **I therefore, a prisoner for the Lord, beg you to lead a life worthy of the calling to which you have been called, with all lowliness and meekness, with patience, forbearing one another in love** (vv. 1-2).

That sounds a lot like Jesus, doesn't it? And, according to how Jesus describes himself, as being one with the Father, it sounds a lot like God.

God, who could destroy us, comes to us in lowliness and meekness and humility, opening up space for us.

"In a roomful of His followers, where their insecurities were dividing them, the same way they divide us, Jesus comes in and washes their feet and messes up the system," Reuben says. "What was a terrible word—'lowliness'—became a good word because it describes how God comes."

The only lifestyle that goes along with being holy and participating in the cause of God is one of voluntary poverty, as Henri Nouwen calls it. A deliberate laying down of our fullness to listen and hear and care.

When we do that, we can *really* listen to one another. More importantly, we can *really* listen to Jesus. As you'll discover in the following excerpt, there's a lot we don't need to listen to anymore. We don't need to listen to a culture that caters to our false sense of pride and ego to say, "You owe this to yourself." And we don't need to listen to a false construct of God that fills us with guilt and shame over things that didn't matter that much to God in the first place. And we don't need to listen to doctrines about God that do more dividing than they do uniting. And we don't need to listen to empty promises.

The best thing we can do is listen to Jesus. There's a word from Him for us today in the following pages.

How Do We Get There?

*W*hat do we mean when we say that Jesus is *the Way?* We know that He points the way for us—but He is more than a *way-pointer.* He doesn't give us directions and disciplines for our journey to God. He is not like the gurus of Oriental religions who share the secrets of their enlightenment and point the way to the god at the top of the mountain. He is more than the way to God in the sense that Shakespeare is the way to poetry or Francis of Assisi is the way to the living of the serving life. We are closer to the truth when we say that *Jesus goes with us on the way; He is our Companion on the journey.*

I'm thinking of a verse of an old gospel song:

> *He will give me grace and glory ...*
> *And go with me, with me all the way.*
>
> —E. W. Blandy

It could be, you know, that adherents to Oriental religions aren't the only ones who put God on top of the mountain and view Him as a goal to be achieved or an end to be realized.

I remember a long time ago, when Mary Jo and I were pastoring a church in Honolulu, a young mother who attended said, "Reverend, when I get good enough, I'm going to become a Christian and join your church." And I'm wondering right now if there is anyone reading these words who is saying, "When I get strong enough, I'm going to enter the victorious life." "When I am good enough, I'm going to be the Christian I want to be." "When I am what I ought to be, then I will feel worthy to come to God." *Jesus has a word for us right here!* The good news of the gospel is that the God of the mountain comes all the way down to where we are and says: *Let me walk with you.*

Thank God, there is no reaching up to find Him. There is no uphill journey to reach Him. He is not up there calling out: "Come on up! It's beautiful up here!" In infinite, caring love He comes all the way to where we are and becomes the loving, strengthening Companion on our journey. But Jesus, the Way, means even more than this. He is more than the *Way-Pointer;* He is more than the Companion *on the way*; HE *IS* THE WAY!

Somewhere in the past, while teaching Greek, I discovered that the word translated *way* is also the word for *road. This fact has given me a whole new dimension to what Jesus said about himself.*

To me, the word *way* is a stained-glass word. It belongs in a church. Let's put a stained-glass window in the church. *Can you see it?* There is the crown, the flames, the dove. There are the beautiful muted colors and symbols. Woven throughout is the banner in Old English letters: **I am the way, and the truth, and the life** (John 14:6). (I can even see the plaque.) *Donated in loving memory of...* Somehow the word *road* doesn't fit in that window very well! It belongs where our lives are lived. It belongs to the path we walk, the sidewalks of our towns and cities, the streets and highways of our busy world. I profoundly believe that Jesus meant His Word to be understood precisely where our real lives are lived.

I read this somewhere: Jesus did not say, "At the end of the way, there you will find Me." He said, *"I am the very Road under your feet!"* That means that, wherever you are, He is there. If you are on a mountain, He is there. If you are in the valley, He is there. If you are in the pit, He is there. *He is the Road under your feet!*

Can we ever believe that we do not have to come to where He is? *He is where we are.* Can we ever trust that we do not have to reach up to grasp Him? *He is the Road under our feet!*

Will anyone ever read these words who feels that God is too far away to be found? Life too messed up to be straightened out? The failure patterns too deeply set to be broken? The entanglements too complex to be solved? The goal so distant that there is no use to try? *Don't believe it! That is the devil's lie!*

I am not talking about how you feel; I am not talking about what is complicating your life. I just want you to know that *Jesus is where you are right now*—feeling what you are feeling, thinking what you are thinking, experiencing what you are experiencing—where you are, as you are, what you are, *right now!*

I think Augustine understood this and spoke the words we all need to hear: "I do not say to thee, Seek a way; the Way Himself has come to thee; arise and walk!"

Bearing Fruit

Maybe it's because I grew up on the farm, but the idea of bearing fruit is very appealing to me. Whatever it means, I want to be a fruitful person. I'm realizing that I don't know much about "bearing fruit." *How do we define it?* Gal. 5:22-23 defines the **fruit of the Spirit** in terms of **love, joy, peace, pa-**

tience, kindness, goodness, faithfulness, gentleness, self-control.

Paul speaks of **bearing fruit in every good work and increasing in the knowledge of God** (Col. 1:10) and of **being filled with the fruits of righteousness** (Phil. 1:11, KJV). Maybe fruit bearing means reproduction in kind—as in orange trees reproducing oranges or people reproducing other people or Christians reproducing Christians.

However defined, whether it refers to growth in grace or productivity or maturity or life or joy or juice or abundance or increase . . . *whatever it is, I want it! And you do, too!* We know this much: Jesus was a fruitful person. And His great concern was for the fruitfulness of the infant Body of Believers to whom He poured out His heart that night. In this paragraph Jesus speaks of several things that seem to be intimately related to fruit bearing. For one thing, Jesus says that fruit bearing involves submission to the pruning process.

I grew up in central California on a citrus ranch. My dad raised oranges and lemons. I never learned much about pruning! When we lived in Pasadena and had a few grapevines, the pruning projects were usually disastrous—no fruit the next year, then very small fruit the following year. But I recall that our pruning of the citrus trees was for two reasons: one was to cut away the dead branches that had been frost-bitten during the

God wants to teach us that the things we let go are no less significant for our fruitfulness than the things we grasp and keep!

winter; the other was to cut out the suckers that looked lush and green but drained the precious life juices from the trees and kept them from producing any fruit. I guess grapes are pruned for the same reasons. Fruit is produced on new growth; the old branches hinder the flow of life to the new stock. As my old granddad would say: *Are you catching on?*

God wants to teach us that the things we let go are no less significant for our fruitfulness than the things we grasp and keep! Did you ever have a garage sale—or need to have one? *Come to think of it, those are two very foolish questions!*

At school one day, one of the professors told of a famous ichthyologist who knew the names of thousands of fish. But he came to a time in his life when he discovered that if he learned the name of a new student, he forgot the name of an old fish!

I think I understand that. Most of the time, my garage is in that condition—if anything *new* goes in, something *old* has got to go out! Sometimes the parting is painful! We finally sold our tandem bike. I bought it for Mary Jo and me to have fun on and stay healthy with. I rode on the front; she rode on the back. *She never did comment much on the view!* And we rode that bike just enough to get sore! Legs hurt too much to stand! Bottoms hurt too much to sit!

I hung it in the garage with nylon rope and pulleys, and it collected dust and seldom came down. It was painful—but it really needed to go. Like other things, it not only cluttered the garage but also cluttered our minds and used up psychic energy. Every time we saw that bike, though no words were spoken, both thoughts and emotions were stirred. *Are we going to ride it? When? Where? Why? Why not?* Defensive thoughts! Conflicting emotions! It was painful, but it really needed to go!

What a small *thing.* Yet the bike became the symbol for all the other *things:* boats, trailers, tools, clothes, and so on. We keep spending, gathering up, holding on . . . We gather things and collect activities until we are too busy to use our gathered things *or get another job to pay for them!* We pick up attitudes and habits and relationships that draw off our energies and sap our strength and then wonder why we aren't joyful and growing and productive. I'm thinking, too, about things we read, things we watch, things we think about. I am wondering about some folks—do they ever, ever have other thoughts than thoughts of sports or making money or buying things?

I am thinking about our spiritual concepts—our ideas of God, the Bible, church. How many of us have minds and hearts filled with childhood's leftover notions—cluttered with outmoded concepts, outgrown hurts, obsolete perceptions? And as the clutter grows, there is no room for fresh, new, understanding attitudes—new fruit! *You know, we really do need a garage sale!*

The Greek word for **prune** in John 15:2 is the same word for **clean** in verse 3. In English the word is *catharsis.* (You don't suppose that's why they call *prunes prunes,* do you? *Surely not!*)

Show Us the Father

I'm wondering if I'm writing to anyone who, like Philip, has known about God for years but has not really known Him as Father. I wonder if behind the God-words, underneath the God-talk, there is a hungering *unknowing* of the Father. That unknowing takes the shape of dissatisfaction and unfulfillment that haunts your days and surrounds your times of devotion. *How sad to know God-language without*

knowing God as Father! When you come right down
to it, the joy, the satisfaction, the authority, the confidence—all these things that we need and want are intimately related to our real fellowship with God *as
our Father.* Hiding underneath Philip's request was
the question, "What is God like?" I am coming to believe more certainly than ever in my life that this is
the fundamental question for all of us.

The fundamental question for folks like us is not,
"Does God exist?" We believe that He exists. We may
have our moments of doubting and unfeeling and
wondering. We have our questions as we face the
mystery of our humanness and the reality of evil and
the sometimes absurd, irrational events of our lives.

But these times are not permanent. We come
back to our moorings. Our faith is pretty well an-
chored in the reality of God. But we do have a problem about God. *And I think it is a very serious one.*

Our question is, "What is God like?" I think there
is no way to tell you how important I think that question is! And I am not so naive as to assume that all of
us have the same quality of understanding. Many of
us, brought up in the care and teaching of the church,
have some ideas about God that *are positively weird!*

Can it be that our ideas of God grow that way?
I've wondered if maybe we all have a sort of spiritual
Polaroid camera with which we take snapshots of
certain events or situations in our lives and thereby
gather up our ideas of God.

When we lived in Pasadena, we had a family
room with a bulletin board on one wall. We tacked
and pinned all kinds of things on that board: the cat
and dog sleeping together like friends, Rob's basket-
ball team, Susan's choir pictures, snaps from our last
vacation, an invitation to a wedding—all these formed
a friendly collage of family "stuff." When we moved in-

to our house in San Diego, we gave the whole thing a little more class. We selected some better family pictures, had them framed, and hung them on the wall in style. The friendly "junk stuff" ended up stuck to the refrigerator with magnets!

I've been thinking that somewhere in the back room of the soul, there must be a bulletin board labeled GOD. Through the years, we have collected various impressions—sermon phrases, Bible stories, life events, crisis times—and tacked them to the board in what has become a collage of our God-image.

A tragedy happens in a godly family. Click! *Why did God let that happen? A bad picture goes on the board.* You read the Old Testament story of Moses and Pharaoh, get the idea that God hardened Pharaoh's heart, then turned around and clobbered him for it. Click! *What's going on here? Another negative picture.* A father beats his children. Click! Someone in church gets sick and everyone prays, but the prayed-for person dies. Click! Someone in church gets sick. Everyone prays and the person recovers. Click! *That's better!* Someone has a remarkable conversion experience. Click! Click! *That's much better!* A church member starts tithing and gets rich! *All right, Lord! And we use a whole roll of film!*

Love God. Trust God. Obey God. Give everything to God. The collage is balancing out, and the big words are sounding better. Can we see what is happening? We are gathering up data from the experiences of our lives and constructing our own ideas of God out of them. *How tragic!* If our lives are good— our God is good. If our lives are bad—our God is bad.

All of us know someone who has said something like this: "Don't talk to me about God! My mother got sick and I prayed for her to be healed. But God didn't care—and she died. Don't talk to me about God!"

On the other hand, there are those whose view of God is shallow and sentimental: "He is so wonderful because He answers all my prayers and solves all my problems and gives me so much happiness." *I wonder what they say when trouble comes?*

It makes all the difference *what we think of God.* It makes all the difference *where we get our ideas of God.* It is one thing to gather up data and develop our own image of God. It is quite another to allow God to *reveal himself* in a self-portrait—His Son, our Lord Jesus.

Well, what sorts of pictures do you have on your board? Will you let the Holy Spirit clear them away and replace them with a picture of the New Testament Jesus? Or are you holding on to God-pictures that are inaccurate and destructive—childhood images, adolescent memories, outdated mementos? These images are so often false and distorted that it is impossible to see God as He wants to be seen—in the person of Jesus Christ. Everything, in the final analysis, hangs on this one peg: God *is like Jesus!*

I'm hearing again the big words: Love God. Trust God. Obey God. Give everything to God. If God is like Jesus, then they are the good words, the beautiful words, the life-transforming words. And to them—and to the Christlike God—my heart is saying, Yes! Yes! Yes!

What Is Your Glory?

I've wondered for a long time about the meaning of this message from Jesus: **The glory which thou hast given me I have given to them, that they may be one even as we are one** (John 17:22). As I think about this verse, I have begun to discover a strange dichotomy. On the one hand, our glory is that which gives us meaning and weight and substance and value and worth and radiance and clout. On the other hand, those are the very things that divide and fragment and separate us. *You know why? Because our glory* becomes *our turf.*

Don't ask me to define that term. All I know is that when I'm on my turf, and the opposition gets a little close, I become defensive. There is an awesome word of Jesus in John 5:44: **How can you believe, who receive glory from one another and do not seek the glory that comes from the only God?** Think about that. It's a fascinating set of dynamics. You see, if I'm a red-hot ukulele player (and I am!), and nobody knows about it, then how will I get my clout? But if I perform and you happen to be a better ukulele player, I am threatened and this separates and divides us.

Jesus said, **The glory which thou hast given me . . .** What was Jesus' glory? What was it that gave Him His meaning and value and authority and confidence and radiance? I don't get the feeling that His glory was in what He wore. **Foxes have holes, and birds of the air have nests; but the Son of man has nowhere to lay his head** (Matt. 8:20).

He had some good people around Him, but I doubt that His clout was in His ability to direct and choose personnel. One of His followers betrayed Him and one of them denied Him, and the whole bunch took off under pressure. (Individually, they weren't anything special.)

I know that He was a great preacher-teacher, and if I know anything about that at all, I'm sure there was a sense of joy and fulfillment in sharing. Yet during the most popular phase of His ministry, there was an underlying deep disappointment because the people weren't seeing what there was to see or hearing what there was to hear.

Wherein, then, was Jesus' glory? I have come to believe that it was in His total dependency upon His Father. Throughout His life, He said, "I came not to do my own will, but the will of my Father. The words that I say I don't say of myself but of the Father who dwells in me and does His work. What I do I do not of myself. I do not seek the glory that comes from men" (see John 6:38; 14:10; 8:28, 50). Jesus' glory was in the totality of His dependence upon His Father, His obedience to His Father, His utter trust in His Father, His profound awareness that in all the affairs of life, His Father was in control.

Now what I am thinking is that if my glory is something I can *do,* that's really fine until somebody comes along *who can do it better!* If my glory is in who I *know,* who I cotton to, then I am dependent upon those people *who might let me down!* So I live defensively, with tension and stress and fear. But if I yield my glories to God so that what gives me my sense of worth and value is not what I can do or what I have or who I know—if my glory is in my relationship with my Father, my total dependence upon Him—*then* when someone comes along who has more books than I have or who has read more of them or who can

Isn't it weird that, seemingly, the very gifts of the Spirit intended to make it possible for us to be what we are and do what we do and develop unity in the Body are the things that so easily divide us?

preach better than I can, *it doesn't hurt quite as much for quite as long!* I think that's what makes it possible in part for us to **maintain the unity of the Spirit in the bond of peace** amidst the diversity of gifts from the Body (Eph. 4:3).

Consider the matter of gifts and ministries. Perhaps many people would have a more benevolent attitude toward the gifts thing and the charismatic thing and the tongues thing *if they were not so divisive!* That's one of my own personal hassles about it, and, naturally, I see myself to be a person of understanding and tolerance and acceptance! *I just wish these things were not so divisive!*

Isn't it weird that, seemingly, the very gifts of the Spirit intended to make it possible for us to be what we are and do what we do and develop unity in the Body are the things that so easily divide us? Maybe it's because there is a subtle shift from total dependence upon God to dependence upon the gift so that my value, meaning, worth, radiance, and clout are found in what I can do, not what God has done for me.

Jesus' glory was tied to the depths of His surrender to His Father. When the crowds flattered Him, He didn't lose His poise. When they rejected Him, He didn't lose His nerve. When they crucified Him, He didn't lose His love! *Somewhere in here, folks, there is a cross!*

Of course there is a fundamental human need for self-worth and meaning. Everyone needs to be able to do something. *I hope you can do something.* It's terrible to grow up feeling like: "I can't do anything." "I ain't nobody." "Nobody cares." That's a bummer all the way. I know and recognize the need *for* a sense of self-worth and self-confidence and self-acceptance. It's just that when those things become the basis of our being, the ground of our glory, it's all up for grabs!

But if I take my glories to the Cross, I can use them or not use them without being personally destroyed and without dividing the Body.

What "Holy" Means

Our religion has a tendency to move toward spirituality and away from the world. Somehow Jesus was able to keep both right where they belong. *How was He able to accomplish this?* What is it that our Lord wants for His Church that is in the world and not of it? Let me gather some scriptures from this 17th chapter of John that at least point us toward the answer: **Sanctify them in the truth; thy word is truth. As thou didst send me into the world, so I have sent them into the world. And for their sake I consecrate myself, that they also may be consecrated in truth** (vv. 17-19). The prayer of Jesus for His in-the-world Church is that it be holy; His heart's desire for us real-world type people is that we be holy.

Now let me talk a little bit about that. I wish all our English words related to the word *holy* had the same sound. All the Greek words for *holy* have a basic sound similarity because they come from one Greek word: *hagios.* I wish there were a single sound in our language for all the words that cluster around the idea of holy. For instance, we have the Anglo-Saxon word family *holy.* Another word in this family is *holiness,* and we ought to have *holify* and *holification!*

There is another group of words from the Latin word family that has an entirely different sound. *Sanctify, sanctification, sanctity,* and we need another one here—*sanct!* I think I like that word.

I really wish we could add these words to our vocabulary, because I believe that words like *sanctification* and *holiness* have become technical terms understood only by the initiated. These terms are often flown like banners, handled as symbols of authority or status symbols.

I may be exaggerating slightly, but I perceive that some of these words like *sanctification* and *holiness* and *redemption,* which at one time were profoundly relevant, which were precious and beautiful life-words, have, for many people, lost their luster and much of their beauty and magnetism.

Do I make myself clear? Some of these precious words—these life-words—one time had juice in them; they had stuff in them; they connected things; they denoted things; they were glorious words; they were magnetic words. But for many, they have lost something; the juice has dried up and they have be-come technical terms, and maybe shibboleths. *And right or wrong, good or bad, that is partly true for me as well!*

At the same time, I see something else going on in the world where I live. While some of the old terms have lost their luster, I perceive that there is a growing, deep-heart *hunger to be holy!* I believe that with all my soul! Maybe this is the hunger to which all other hungers are related. Maybe this fundamental hunger to be holy is that God-shaped vacuum in the heart of every person. And, oddly enough, though that hunger persists, it is seldom expressed.

I don't know if we can find new terms, new lan-guage, new lingo that would help us, but I know that there is within us a hunger to be holy. And I know that the heart hunger of our Lord for His Church is that the people of God be **sanctified, and [made] meet for the master's use** (2 Tim. 2:21, KJV).

What does it mean to be holy? I'd like to take the lid off on my own journey of understanding. It seems to me that at the end of the articles and at the end of the journal studies and at the end of the textbook studies on the idea of holiness, one idea emerges: *To be holy means to be different by virtue of belonging to God.*

The first big word in that sentence is the word *belonging.* You see, only God is holy in any original and underived sense. *Only God* in His separateness, His otherness, His purity, His wholeness *is holy. Only God is "sanct."* Other things or persons or places become holy by virtue of a "holifying" relationship with the God who alone is holy.

That's why the Temple and the vessels in the Temple and the vestments and the oil and all the stuff they used in religious ceremonies could be holy—because they belonged to God. Then what about holy *people?* Fundamentally, in the Bible, people are holy only because they belong to God. In this prayer, Jesus' high-priestly prayer, He asks for our wills, for our hearts to be entirely devoted to God and to His service. All our talents, all our energies, all our lives are to be marked *with the seal of consecration.* I think that's the most beautiful phrase I have heard in a long time—"marked with the seal of consecration." This phrase implies the renouncing of self, just as Jesus was willing to leave heaven and renounce all heavenly claims. *It means a radical belonging to God!*

Look at Israel in the Old Testament. Israel is nothing apart from the initiative and the calling of God. Into the flow of human history comes Israel, called into being by God. I don't know the sources and backgrounds of other nations, but I do know about Abraham. I know about Isaac and Jacob and Joseph. We know what God said to Moses on the back slopes of Mount Horeb. We know that God brought them out of Egypt and made them into a nation at the foot of Sinai. We know that He entered into covenant relationship with them. And God said to them, I didn't call you because you were beautiful or because you were wise or because you were good or because you were big. I set my love upon you and I have called you. And apart from that calling, Israel is nothing and has nothing.

Why was it that the prophets kept warning: "Don't get involved with Assyria." "Don't get involved with Babylon." "Don't put your trust in Egypt." "Trust God!" It wasn't because they were political neutralists. It was because they saw that Israel existed for one reason—their relationship to God. When Israel moved away from that fundamental dependency, they got into trouble.

It doesn't take a whole lot of brains to bring this right over into the New Testament and relate it to the people of the new covenant, the new Israel, the Church of God. Where does the Church come from? We didn't create it. God did! It's His thing! He brought it into being in the New Exodus, consummated on the Cross. Liberated by the power of the Spirit, we move out under the sign of the Cross as the new Israel, the people of God.

And God says to us: I didn't call you because you were good. I didn't call you because you were great. I didn't call you because you were anything special. God does not use us because we are better, bigger, richer, more creative, or more intelligent. The Church is what it is because and only because it belongs to God and has been called into existence by the Word. And, suddenly, we are right in the middle of the New Testament ethic that says to us, "Be what you are." *"Be a God-person."*

Jesus said, you remember, **Apart from me you can do nothing** (John 15:5). To be holy, then, really means to put at the center of our lives what is, in fact, the Center of our lives. *We are to be God-people.*

Holiness means God-centeredness. It means being separated unto Him. It means belonging to a community that is the possession of God.

Holiness means God-centeredness. It means being separated unto Him. It means belonging to a community that is the possession of God.

And when we realize that God is intrinsically holy, we understand why, in the process of moving into holy relationship with Him, we need cleansing, a dying, and a liberation from the power of the carnal mind. And if we are to be persons in a community that belongs to God, we also need the empowering of the Holy Spirit.

I am hearing the words of an old invitation hymn:

Break down every idol; cast out every foe.

—James Nicholson

We are called to be a holy people, a God-people. And as that word penetrates my life, I find that it has increasing power and increasing beauty and increasing magnetism and makes increasing demands and talks to me about what I say I am—*a God-person.*

The second word in our key sentence is *different. Different by belonging.* As with old Israel, so with the new Israel. Old Israel was different from surrounding nations because every part of its life was related to God. The people were to reflect His character and will as spelled out in the Book of the Covenant.

For us of the new covenant, it is no different. Radical belonging issues in lives that reflect God's character and will. *What does that mean for me personally?* It means my life is to be lived in growing likeness to Jesus through the power of His Spirit. That is the expression of radical belonging!

Jesus said, **[Don't] take them out of the world. . . . Sanctify them through thy truth: thy word is truth. As thou hast sent me . . . so have I also sent them. . . . And for their sakes I sanctify myself, that they also might be sanctified through the truth** (John 17:15, 17-19, KJV). When it comes right down to it, holiness means *God-centeredness, Christlikeness,* and *God-sentness.*

And that's the prayer of Jesus for us. In the midst of all this, we are *in* the world, sent *to* the world. And if I'm going to be a person that puts God at the center of my life and proclaims Him to the world, I'll have to do it with the rooms of my house arranged the way they are. I may have to learn to like the dog! I may need to learn how to accept the intrusion of people around me to whom I want to shout: WOULD YOU PLEASE LEAVE ME ALONE SO I CAN BE HOLY?!

Turn it *off!* Take it away! I want to pray! No! The word of the Lord comes to us: **In the world! In the world!** (v. 11). To which we say, "Yes, Lord!" I'm sure you are aware that what is on my heart is really a sharing of some of my own struggles about what it means to be a holy person, so it's hard for me to know where this meets *you.* But I want to tell you that the calling of God is that we be His people. We must turn away from false dependencies and put Him *at the center of our lives!*

As our Lord was preparing His people for His departure, that yearning cry of His heart to His Father was that the people He left behind would be the holy people of God. *I want to be a part of that! And so do you! That's our crowd!*

Oneness

It's been several years now since I had the privilege of becoming chaplain of a Christian college. And I thought when I came to the college that it would probably be heaven on earth in terms of oneness. Look at all the things students have in common: common age-group, common culture, common background, common religious heritage, common socioeconomic status, common ideals and goals. When you consider all the things that should bind people together, surely here we would be one in the Lord!

But I discovered that in the midst of a Christian community of believers, there can be loneliness, fragmentation, judgment, separation, status symbols, and divisions that tear it all up. *Did you know that?* On the campus of this Christian college, after school had been going on for three or four weeks, there was one girl who had not gone to the dining hall yet! *She ate her meals out of the vending things in the dormitory!* She was so lonely; she was so insecure; she was so bound up; *she hadn't even gone to the dining hall yet!*

I'm sure it wouldn't have blessed her a whole lot if I had said, "Your problem is that you're neurotic!" "Oh, thanks! I'll go to the dining hall now!" I discovered something else too. I found that multiplying activities doesn't bring oneness either. In our campus situation we say that if people are lonely and don't get together, we need to have more interdorm parties. Well, we do need more times to get together. But the more parties you have for people to get together, the more occasions there are for the lonely people *to feel more lonely!* The more dating occasions you have, the more misery is compounded with the *undating*.

I'm coming to see that all of those superficial

things that we think will bring us together *don't.*
There is only one thing that will bring us together,
and that is our oneness in the Lord! That's why I am
so concerned and turned on about groups and Bible
studies and prayer fellowships. If you're having them
where you are—good! *Have some more.* If not, *why
not,* and when are you going to start?

We need places to get together around the Word,
and around the Lord, and around our true oneness.
When we are affirming our true oneness, we are, in
fact, being what we are—and that's where the loneliness breaks down; that's where the openness begins;
that's where the joy is! I'm laying this on you as if you
need it, and I'm just going to assume that you do! If
you don't—well, just praise the Lord *and pass it on!* I
am chagrined at the little things that divide us, when,
in truth, the oneness that we have in Christ is the
great reality within the Christian life. What I'm seeing
as I've never seen before is that not only must the little things bow, but also the biggest things of our lives
must bow, *before our oneness in Christ.*

Several years ago, my wife and I had the privilege
of spending some time in Germany, where I spoke to
an American military congregation in Frankfurt. Now
picture this: an American military congregation in
Germany—one family from North Dakota, one family from California, one family from Alabama, one family from Oklahoma, one family from Kansas, one family
from Michigan—each bringing its own perception of
what a Nazarene church ought to be.

So they came thinking, "Well, we're in a strange
land, but praise the Lord. There are a bunch of good
old Nazarenes here!" Lo and behold, when they came
together in the church, they found other perceptions
and other ideas. And so did we! Some wanted old-
fashioned revival preaching, and some wanted en-

counter groups. Some wanted "Holy, Holy, Holy," and some wanted "Do, Lord." Some wanted a guitar, and some wanted an organ. And here they all were—coming from the same denomination with all these different expectations.

And you may not believe this, but this *American* congregation in *Frankfurt, Germany,* was pastored by a wonderful, young *Scottish* preacher who loved his native brogue and who pr-r-reached and pr-r-rayed for the par-r-rishioner-r-rs of his congregation! And the Scottish preacher was married to a *German* girl, which meant that the Americans couldn't gripe about the Germans because the pastor's wife was there! And, to further complicate things, since it was a *military* congregation, there was a lieutenant colonel and a sergeant on the same church governing board. (My guess is that at the board meetings, the sergeant would say, "I move we vote by secret ballot!")

There we were—the gathered Body of Believers. And it was a time of some rich insights for me—a beautiful time of understanding. The Lord began to talk to me about some things—about oneness and fellowship. I'm not sure that we were much blessing to that wonderful group—but they were a blessing to Mary Jo and me! In that group were all the factors that could divide and separate and alienate the Body. *Instead, there was beautiful fellowship.* At the center of the oneness, there was an awareness of the Cross on which our prejudices, expectations, anticipations, desires were nailed for the sake of oneness of the life and the Body. I remembered what Paul said: **There is neither Jew nor Greek, there is neither slave nor free, there is neither male nor female; for you are all one in Christ Jesus** (Gal. 3:28).

As I think now about that verse, I realize that the oneness of the Body is greater than prejudice, rank, sex, expectations, anticipations, nationality! Nationality. That's who we *are!* Have you ever been to a country where another language is spoken almost exclusively? We were getting along pretty well in Germany. I knew a few phrases: *Auf wiedersehen. Entschuldigen Sie!* That means "Good-bye" and "Pardon me!"

Have you ever noticed that when you talk to someone who doesn't speak English, you speak loudly and d-i-s-t-i-n-c-t-l-y! And you feel so frustrated because they still don't understand!

But when Mary Jo and I went down to Frankfurt to do some shopping, we needed some directions, and nobody understood and nobody cared. Do you know what I mean? You get this feeling of desperation and isolation, and they're dumb and stupid—so you talk LOUDER! Have you ever noticed that when you talk to someone who doesn't speak English, you speak loudly and d-i-s-t-i-n-c-t-l-y! And you feel so frustrated because they still don't understand!

Can we lay down our *nationality* before the oneness of the Body? Can we lay down our status—**neither bond nor free?** Can we lay down our sexuality—**neither male nor female?** *God help us male chauvinists, every one!*

How much Jesus cares about this. It is so important to Him that the dominant theme of His heart cry on the night before He died was that we affirm and strengthen that oneness that is ours in the shared life of Christ. Don't let anything *separate* you in your fellowship of believers! Don't let *anything* separate you in your church. Now what was true in the church in Frankfurt is true in the entire Body of Believers. What is it that separates you from those around you? *Whatever it is—it isn't enough!*

Is it denominationalism? Some denominations are conservative. Some are liberal. There are a lot of differences in the fellowship. *But the differences are not enough to separate us!* Is it your lifestyle? Are you struggling to keep up with the Joneses? Are the Joneses struggling to keep up with you? *There is nothing that matters more than our oneness.*

Look again at what Jesus said: **[Make] them . . . one, *so that the world may know*** (John 17:23, emphasis added). If we want to make an impact on our world, those things that separate must bow down! But we're masters at splitting. And we know how to defend our stand *as a matter of principle* to preserve our integrity (meaning, "to protect our ego").

Jesus speaks to that: Don't let anything separate you! Don't speak of compromise! Don't talk about maintaining principle in the midst of division.

I think of our Lord, **who, though he was in the form of God, did not count equality with God a thing to be grasped, but *emptied himself,* taking the form of a servant, being born in the likeness of men** (Phil. 2:6-7, emphasis added). Jesus didn't lay aside what He *had.* He laid aside what He *was. And that speaks to me!* God's will is that we be one. And neither our language nor our culture nor our race nor our heritage—all the things that make us what we are—*must separate us!*

We must ultimately bow at the foot of the Cross so that our oneness in Christ may merge. If the Holy Spirit of oneness would sweep over individual communities of believers until all the superficial barriers were broken down and we would affirm each other and live in our oneness in Christ, the blessing and grace and power of God could be present in ways that we might never dream! And the world would *know*—and the world would *believe!*

Let us bow down now and place on the altar our nationality, our status, our sexuality, our prejudices, *our all!* Let's bow before the Man at the head of the table—*and pass the bread!*

I Vote Yes

"Pass the bread" really means to express our oneness by loving each other! At the very close of the prayer, Jesus said something significant about love: **I will make [thy name] known, that the love with which thou hast loved me may be in them, and I in them** (John 17:26). *God is love. Love is God.*

I believe, too, that love is our felt oneness behaviorized, actualized in practice, manifested in discernible acts of *Christlike caring.* Fundamentally, we *are* one. But if I really *believe* it, I will *behave* it. I will look at you. I will not judge you. If I really know that we are one, I will care for you as a person. I will affirm you. Love is caring for persons as persons, releasing persons, a steadfast refusal to judge. In good, plain English love means "I vote yes on you." Love means, on the basis of our oneness in Christ: I *affirm you. Affirm.* That's a neat word, isn't it?

What it really means is: When the vote is in, I am on the affirmative side. I am *for* you. *I vote yes on you as a person!* That doesn't mean I like everything you do or approve of the way you act. *Not at all.*

Let me put it this way, because sometimes opposites help us to understand concepts. We drive into the church parking lot. Just as we get there, another car parks nearby. We glance over to see who it is. *Oh, no!* We walk into the sanctuary, sit down, and there is that same person! *Oh, no!* We open up the bulletin: Sister So-and-So is singing today. *Oh, no!* Pastor's sermon is on tithing. *Oh, no!*

Meanwhile, back on the home front, the phone rings—pick it up—*Oh, no!* The doorbell rings—open the door—*Oh, no!*

It is also possible for us to develop a no vote on those who are closest to us, isn't it? I know some husbands who are forever saying no to their wives. Every communication is a put-down. I am thinking of a guy who always refers to his wife as "The Wife" (but probably in lowercase, "the wife"). And I feel like saying, "Hello, *The,* how are you?" Just No! No! No!

And there are wives who are always saying no to their husbands. The men can never do anything right. Every story is interrupted seven times! "Honey, it wasn't Tuesday; it was Wednesday." "It wasn't nine o'clock; it was a quarter after." "It wasn't $50; it was $500!" "He didn't win it; he lost it!" You know, he can never ever tell a story right!

Some children are always saying no to their parents. "You don't understand me." "You don't care." "Why can't you be like Marcia's parents?"

And some parents are always saying no to their children. Maybe we think that saying no is the way to love them. We are helping them to become better! "Will you ever be on time?" "Aren't you ever going to grow up?" "When will you ...?" "Why don't you ...?" "When are you going to stop picking your pimples?" I know that dates me. My children can't stand the word *pimples,* and I hate *zits!* Oh, we know how to say no, all right! My grandmother used to say that some people were just "cut on the bias"! No! No! No!

Let's go back now and look at what a loving yes can mean. I won't talk long about this. It is so beautiful that, if I do, you will begin to think you have died and gone to heaven! We are now in the parking lot of the church, and there "he" is, driving up nearby. *Yes!* We are sitting down in church and notice that Sister Smith is going to sing. *Yes!* The pastor gives the call to worship: **I was glad when they said unto me, Let us go into the house of the Lord** (Ps. 122:1, KJV). *Oh, yes!* The room is messy. *Yes!* The story is not quite right. *OK.* (Remember, it does not mean that you approve of or agree with everything.)

It doesn't mean that your heart is not broken by the choices or lifestyles of those you love. It does mean that in your heart you are saying: I love you. You are a person of infinite worth. I say yes to you because we are one. Here's what I believe with all my heart: In that yes, the love of God is present!

Let's go back to Jesus' prayer: **. . . that the love with which thou hast loved me may be in them, and I in them** (John 17:26).

Well, how did the Father love the Son? *The Father said yes to His Son!* At His baptism: **Thou art my beloved Son, with thee I am well pleased** (Mark 1:11). At His transfiguration: **This is my beloved Son; listen to him** (9:7). And, supremely, at the Resurrection, the Father was saying yes to Jesus!

And Jesus said yes to His Father: **My food is to do the will of him who sent me, and to accomplish his work** (John 4:34). **And the word which you hear is not mine but the Father's who sent me** (14:24). **I glorified thee on earth, having accomplished the work which thou gavest me to do** (17:4). **My Father, if it be possible, let this cup pass from me; nevertheless, not as I will, but as thou wilt** (Matt. 26:39). The Father says yes to the Son. The Son says yes to the Father; and in the Son, the Father says yes to us!

There is a marvelous verse in 2 Cor. 1:20: **For all the promises of God find their Yes in him.** In Him, we have the guarantee of all His promises! Right now, someone may be saying no to you. It may seem that the whole world is saying no. But God, in Jesus, is saying *yes!* **He who did not spare his own Son but gave him up for us all, will he not also give us all things with him?** (Rom. 8:32).

God is saying yes to us! What I am thinking is that maybe we better be passing it on—like passing the bread! Here is where it all comes home: The Father's yes and the Son's yes, and the great yes of the promises, are to find their expression in our love *that says yes to each other!*

You know, it's an exciting thing, a scary thing, a wonderful thing to think about this!

What if we really believed that God is saying yes to us, too, and that He won't quit! What if we really believed in each other with a yes love that wouldn't quit! *And what if we just didn't quit loving—no matter what!*

What if someone makes a miserable blunder—and we just don't quit loving him? What if somebody fails—and we keep right on loving him? What if some insecure clown fouls everything up—and we love him anyway? What about the lonely ones, the insecure ones, the unbeautiful ones! Could we, in the community of believers—warmed by the wonderful, undeserved love of God—could we possibly just keep on loving them? Oh, if there is any place like that in this world, I want to be there!

And I am hearing again the word of the Lord, *What are you going to do about loving?* You see, we have no alternative. There are no options. Love is commanded. Therefore, our response must be in the actualizing of our oneness. As we create a nonjudging, affirming, loving atmosphere, what life-changing miracles can happen! What beautiful transformations will take place *when we stop saying no and start reflecting the yes of God in Jesus.*

Well, are you ready to vote? All in favor, say *Yes!*

Who, Me?

Well, I want us to go back one more time and run this high-priestly prayer though our small computer and push the button labeled "they." I find myself increasingly concerned about these "they" verses in which Jesus talks about disciples. *Who, me, Lord?* Are You talking to me? I think so! By the grace of God—I am a disciple! *Are you?* Well, *are you?* If you are, nod your head a little bit. *The Lord may be looking on and would like to know.*

I'm not saying by that we are making any rash statements about ourselves. But I believe that, despite our needs and our weaknesses, by the grace of God WE ARE DISCIPLES! And I think that what Jesus says *about* us, *to* us, is important *for* us.

Let's gather up some of these "they" passages: **They** **have kept thy word** (John 17:6). **Now** *they* **know that everything that thou hast given me is from thee; for I have given them the words which thou gavest me, and** *they* **have received them and know in truth that I came from thee; and** *they* **have believed that thou didst send me**

But Jesus, in these simple statements recorded by John, described His disciples—all of us!

(vv. 7-8). *They* **are thine** (v. 9). *They* **are in the world** (v. 11). *And in case you didn't hear it:* *they* **are not of the world** (v. 16, all emphases added).

If I were to attempt to characterize disciples, *I don't know what I would write down!* But Jesus, in these simple statements recorded by John, described His disciples—all of us! When I summarize these verses, I come up with four basic statements, four things Jesus said about us—really, two pairs of things. One and two: Disciples keep Jesus' words; therefore they know who Jesus is. Three and four: They are in the world, but they belong to God.

We've talked about some of these things in earlier chapters. Now let's put them all together! Taking it from the top, Jesus said that disciples keep His words; therefore they know who He is. When I was in the process of working through John 17 and trying to learn it and read it and outline it and memorize it and get it into a thinkable, talkable form, I started working through these "they" sections.

I made a list, and I started at the top just as naturally and instinctively as anything in the world. *Disciples know who Jesus is; therefore they keep His words.* I wrote that down just as nicely as could be.

Then I went on to the other verses. But I kept going back to those first verses and thinking about them, and I read the prayer again, and do you know what I discovered? I found that my natural, instinctive order of things was *totally reversed!* I had written, *Disciples know; therefore they obey.* But that order is precisely reversed in this prayer and in the New Testament itself. *Disciples obey; therefore they know!*

Do you know what we are prone to do? We try too often to convince people who Jesus *is,* what He has done, what He stands for, and we come on in a teaching, doctrinal, defensive, or sometimes, unfortunately, *offensive* way. When I began to see what the order really is, it was such a relief! Because if you have to convince people who Jesus is before you can get them to obey, you've got to be a lot smarter than the people you talk to!

As wise as we are, that does somewhat limit the field, doesn't it? And it's a marvelous thing just to relax in the understanding that we do not have to have all the answers! Our task is not to meet the objections and questions of all comers, but to begin at the point of obedience and not at the point of full understanding. So the thing that's been so great in my own life is simply to understand that I do not have to begin with the assurance of who Jesus is and then come to obedience; rather, if I will obey, I will come to understand! *There is absolutely no way to communicate to you the depth of the revelation that that concept has brought about in my life!*

Listen again to Jesus: **I have given them the words which thou gavest me, and they have received them and know in truth that I came from thee; and they have *believed* that thou didst send me** (John 17:8, emphasis added). *The point of beginning is the point of obedience!* I really do believe that!

Do you suppose that when those first people met Jesus, they knew all about Him? When Jesus first encountered the men who later followed Him, I don't believe they knew who He was completely. I think they knew a little bit. They had been together in an intimate fellowship, but they did not understand all about Jesus. They didn't know about the shepherds, the star, the manger, the angel. They didn't know about those things. They didn't know about "the other wise man." They hadn't heard about "the littlest angel." They knew nothing about the little "drummer boy." No awareness of *Amahl and the Night Visitors. I marvel that they could get saved at all!*

Lovers of myth we are. The first followers didn't

know all these things, but they began to follow and listen and hear! Through days and weeks and months, they began to say yes!

I love this line: **I have given them the words which thou gavest me, and they have *received* them** (emphasis added). *Received.* Isn't that a beautiful word? They have *received* them. They have *let them in.* They have *come to know!*

Then one day Jesus took the disciples up north to Caesarea Philippi and said to them: **Who do you say that I am?** (Matt. 16:15). Peter answered first, of course: **You are the Christ, the Son of the living God** (v. 16). And Jesus said: **Blessed are you, Simon Bar-Jona! For flesh and blood has not revealed this to you, but my Father who is in heaven** (v. 17). Here is a revelation of God that did not come at the beginning, *but in the middle.*

It came as a result of days and weeks and months of following, responding, obeying, listening, hearing; and, gradually, there was that beautiful dawning when the Holy Spirit opened up to them *who Jesus really was!*

Assurance does not begin with our relationship with Christ. It is really the growing bottom line to our obedience. Wherever you are on your journey, if there is doubt and confusion and misunderstanding, and you're trying to figure out what's what, who's who, what's the gospel all about, what's dumb, what really matters, what's cultural, what's right, who is Jesus, what's He all about—*I think there is a word of the Lord for us.*

As we begin to obey, we will come to growing assurance and certainty! *I believe that with all my heart!* We want some experience to lift us up like the tide and set us down in a world of confident assurance!

We want a gospel *experience* that brings us the emotion and joy that eliminate doubts and questions. We want that. May I repeat what I wrote earlier in the book? It is *very* important to me these days of my journey. I'm learning that maybe we don't need some great experience. We've already had that. What we really need is genuine, careful, deliberate *obedience to what we know!*

So when I talk about obedience, I'm not really talking about what we can't understand and what we can't do. I'm not talking about those words of Jesus that are too much for us. What bothers me are the words that are *understandable* and *doable!* What is disturbing to me in my own life is that it is so difficult to let the words of Jesus come down into my daily conversations, my daily patterns of thoughts and response and reaction. Words like **Judge not** (Matt. 7:1). Words like **Do not be anxious** (6:25). Words that say, "You don't have to retaliate" (see 5:38-39). Words like **Take up [your] cross and follow me** (16:24). Words that tell me, "When you go to a banquet, don't go wandering around the head table looking for your name. Just go in and sit down at the end somewhere. If they want you, they'll come and get you" (see Luke 14:8-10).

Now the worst part of those words that I have given to you from Jesus *is that I understand them.* I just understand them. I don't understand all about them. I have to have my own safety hatch, but I understand them. *Don't you?*

The marvelous thing about it is that as we begin to obey in just the little things, the little-big things, our assurance grows, our certainty grows. Elton Trueblood said: "The eyes of the soul are washed by obedience." *I think I believe that.*

Now I'm not saying that all of our doubts and all

of our problems and all of our hassles with the Christian faith come from doubt and disobedience—*just most of them.*

It's just amazing how often underneath the points of uncertainty and confusion and doubt there is a closing of the eyes or a turning away from something we know we really ought to do! So much is solved by our simple, honest obedience to Jesus! That's a hard word, but a good word. It's a word of judgment, but a word of hope.

I read about the young skeptic who loved to discourse with the guru who lived in a hut at the top of a mountain. The skeptic said: "Father, come out. I would talk with you about my doubts." The old saint replied: "Son, come in. I would talk with you about your sins." *But that's a word of hope, isn't it?*

I believe profoundly that when you begin to obey, you begin to grow in security, in assurance, in confidence about who Jesus is. *What a privilege to know Jesus!*

Do you know what Christian people say at a funeral or in a hospital? They say, "I wonder what people do who don't know the Lord!" *That's what we say to each other, isn't it?* What *do* people do without Jesus?

I think about all the lonely people in the midst of

the masses. . . . I think about our industrialized, depersonalized, affluent, capitalistic society that has left
deep, black chasms and aching voids in the hearts of
people. I think about those people trying to fill those
voids and those chasms *with so many things that
won't fit!* The occult, communes, sex cults, violence
cults, Satan worship, witches, and warlocks! *Can you
believe that those are good, contemporary nouns?* I
didn't even know what a warlock was until I watched
Bewitched on TV. I never heard of this stuff. But it's
here. It's a part of our culture, and *it's scary!*

Then there is astrology. Think of all the millions
of dollars spent on that stuff! I want you to know I
don't believe in all that. *I'm a Scorpio and I'm skepti-
cal!*

During these times of our lives, these times of
seething internal currents, these times of worldwide
crisis and chaos—*we have a word!* That word is the
teaching of Jesus. At the heart of our world there is an
Anchor, a Rock, a Savior!

What a rock we have in Jesus!

And that beautiful knowledge of Him does not
belong exclusively to the few who happen to have
the right personality or the right "genes and cor-
duroys" or have had a fantastic experience!

Of course, I thank God for those who have had
"fantastic" experiences. I talked with a guy at school
one time who had been wallowing around in a life of
sin. He had wandered and searched—trying to find
himself. He had a mother who prayed for him. And he
said he had a vision that Jesus came to where he was
and talked to him. He tried to talk himself out of what
he had seen, but the vision wouldn't go away. It was a
radical, transforming vision, and it was real.

That's great, but I don't know what that is. I never did see anything like that. I've got no data to han-

dle a thing like that. It doesn't compute. Most of us come to this beautiful knowledge of Jesus not by some out-of-this-world experience but by *simple, honest obedience.* I'm thinking of Judas, not Iscariot, who asked: **Lord, how is it that you will manifest yourself to us, and not to the world?** Jesus said, **If a man loves me, he will *keep my word, and my Father will love him, and we will come to him and make our home with him*** (John 14:22-23, emphasis added). *Isn't that beautiful? Just like that!*

I'm thinking of a story that I've heard all my life. Jesus told it at the end of the Sermon on the Mount. **A wise man . . . built his house upon the rock.** *Remember the story?* **And the rain fell, and the floods came, and the winds blew and beat upon that house, but it did not fall, because it had been founded on the rock. And every one who hears these words of mine and does not do them will be like a foolish man who built his house upon the sand; and the rain fell, and the floods came, and the winds blew and beat against that house, and it fell; and great was the fall of it** (Matt. 7:24-27).

I've heard those words all of my life, and after all these years, *I'm beginning to hear them!* In times like these, we need an anchor that grips the solid Rock!

Well, how do you build on a rock? How do you know that your life has been made secure? What is the key to that stability that can outlast the rain, the winds, the flood? *Hearing and doing the words of Jesus. Just like that!* I don't know about you, but this whole thing meets me right where I am, with my needs, my struggles, my desires *for the rest of my life!*

I care what happens to me *the rest of my life.* It isn't going to be that long! I have no desire to die on the vine. I don't want to go Blah! until I die. I really do care what happens to me in the next 20 years. Do you? Yes, you do! Where is newness for *me?* Shall I wait around for some holy zap?

Where are *you?* Are you waiting for Jesus to come to the foot of the bed? What will be the source of certainty in our lives? What will be the base for understanding, insight, growth? *I think I know. It's the same for me as for thee.* As you and I listen to, and respond to, and obey THE WORDS OF JESUS, my life will be built on the rock, *and so will yours.*

Are you listening? Am I listening? Jesus has some words for us.

~ 4 ~

The Temptations of Jesus

Dean Nelson

My first job out of college was with a large metropolitan church in Detroit. I was assigned two areas, and one of them was to manage a Christian coffeehouse that the church owned. It was a very 1970s thing for churches to do during that era of postfolk but pre-heavy metal music.

The facility was about a mile from the church building—the kind of place where you'd expect to see Bob Dylan or Peter, Paul, and Mary play on a weekend. The period was at the very front end of the contemporary Christian music scene, and we had a full house each night to see the various groups as they passed through town. Some of the musicians are still around. Most, mercifully, have found other avenues of fulfillment.

The other area I worked with was the youth group of the church. It was a group, by the way, that did not mix with the coffeehouse gang. One group was more upper-class and came from generations of churchgoers, and the other came literally off the streets. Some in the coffeehouse gatherings had never even heard of Jesus. Ministry to the two groups couldn't have been more different.

The result was a type of identity crisis within myself. I didn't feel that I was doing all that well with either group, and I wondered why ministry couldn't just be ministry regardless of the group and why I didn't know more about ministry than I did.

I felt ineffective, pulled between the affluent and the poor, and wondered why nothing I tried in either area seemed to be working. I believed that I knew how ministry was measured in this culture and how success was defined. I was not measuring up; the numbers weren't keeping pace with other similar metropolitan churches. Members of the church board wondered why we weren't growing like those other churches.

Some friends who were also in youth ministry told me about a retreat coming up for youth ministers from several denominations. It sounded like a great time of fellowship and personal renewal, so I went. The speakers were nationally known as experts in the field of youth ministry and youth culture.

Another speaker was Reuben Welch. He spoke on the temptations of Jesus and how real they were for Jesus and how real those same temptations are for us today. Just as it felt when I first heard him a few years before, this was some of the greatest and most liberating news I had ever heard. Those talks then became the powerful little book *The Temptations of Jesus: His Victory and Ours.*

In the gentle-yet-forceful, funny-yet-painfully-poignant way that he has, Reuben made it clear that these temptations of Jesus were not just a little three-act drama played out in the presence of rodents, jackals, gophers, snakes, and lizards in the high desert. He made it clear that this was not a show where the good guy wins and the bad guy loses and, as the curtain closes, Satan slinks away defeated and Jesus marches away triumphant.

Jesus was tempted throughout His life, but it was after His baptism, while in the wilderness, where who He was and what He was to do were deeply searched and tested. Underneath each of the temptations were two fundamental issues.

"First," Reuben told us, "He was tempted to doubt the validity of the Father's word to Him."

The word was spoken at His baptism: "This is my beloved Son, with whom I am well pleased" (Matt. 3:17).

His first temptation was to ask, "Am I really who I think I am?" This is how Jesus' temptation is important to us today—when we ask ourselves, "Are we who we say we are?" That's another way of saying, "Can I really believe that God loves me?" Jesus was tempted to doubt the Father's word to Him about who He was. In the middle of my own period of wondering how God viewed me and my dwindling effectiveness in Detroit, I heard that Jesus was tempted to doubt the validity of His relationship with God.

I believe we all tend to wonder about this. Even Adam and Eve were confronted with this when the serpent said, "You don't really think God meant what He said, do you?" (see Gen. 3:1, 4-5). So when we know that Jesus was tempted, as we are, we know we have One who has completely entered into our human experience to love us and heal us and reconcile us to God, and we have One who won victory over this temptation. Because of Christ in us, His victory is our victory. This is what I was picking up from Reuben during this retreat.

"We can share in the victory that our Lord won there at the times in our lives of failure or distress or testing or bleakness or barrenness or aloneness," he said. "What's the fundamental issue? Don't let go of your faith in the Father. His word to us is true."

"That's where we're tempted, too, isn't it? To turn away from the path of servanthood and suffering to find some other way to fulfill the Father's purpose."

There was a second temptation Jesus faced that also connected with the ministers gathered at that retreat center.

"I believe that in every temptation Jesus faced, there was the fundamental temptation to turn away from the path of suffering love, to which His Father had called Him," Reuben said. "That's where we're tempted, too, isn't it? To turn away from the path of servanthood and suffering to find some other way to fulfill the Father's purpose."

All of us in the room knew what he was talking about. We had all subjected our youth groups to programs, formulas, and proven methods for ministry in hopes of reaching "success." We also knew we would be faced with this temptation the rest of our lives, the way Jesus was. It seemed overwhelming.

But the good news was that Jesus' victory over the idol of success is our victory too. Because of Jesus' victory in the wilderness, because of Reuben's insightful way of showing us how this victory is ours, the youth ministers' retreat became a victory celebration. Discouraged and alienated ministers who considered themselves failures brought their broken selves out of their own "wilderness" and experienced victory and hope in Christ. It was a defining moment for many of us.

There are at least two ironies out of this experience. One is that I went back to Detroit, resigned as an associate pastor, and entered the field of journalism. It felt just as incongruous then as it may seem to a reader now. But it was the right move for everyone, perhaps especially for those two groups I worked with in Detroit! I knew that I was not abandoning my call to fulfilling my Father's purpose, but I had become convinced that the Detroit arrangement was at best a temporary one.

The other irony out of this time is that Reuben took these messages directly from our conferences to a retreat a very large Evangelical church was conducting. The messages, which were overwhelmingly well received during his first delivery, were just as overwhelmingly rejected by the group.

"This was the first time I had encountered a superchurch," Reuben said. "They felt that they were experiencing all of the blessings of God because they had thousands of people attending. They said, 'Look—we have our services on TV!' They were using commercial means to measure their success, which I thought was a problem."

He began talking to them about Jesus turning away from the temptation of power and success and choosing the path of servanthood that led to the Cross.

What that group was not willing to accept was that there was something more important than whether their church did well. What happened in the wilderness with Jesus was that He made a fundamental shift in the center of gravity of His life, away from himself to God, Reuben said. He did not have to do anything after that but to obey the Father.

"Jesus settled the issue of success and survival—for himself and for us," Reuben said. "Once He settled the matter that He did not have to survive, He was free to give, to love, to obey, to respond, to not respond, to stay, to leave—with incredible freedom, incredible authority, awesome integrity, marvelous power."

Rather than figuring out a way to make sure an organization or institution or a movement survives, Jesus' victory gives us the freedom to simply bear witness to the truth.

Rather than figuring out a way to make sure an organization or institution or a movement survives, Jesus' victory gives us the freedom to simply bear witness to the truth—that we are called and loved by God, and that we are to adopt a life of servanthood. That's the message Jesus got at His baptism, that's what He clung to in the wilderness during the time of temptation at His weakest points, and that's the victorious place where we can live too.

Reuben has thought about this. His own "success" as a teacher, writer, chaplain, and preacher was limited, one could say, by a daughter in an institution who needed him and Mary Jo nearby.

"She was a type of tether for us," he said. "We needed to be around her, and that kept me from too much of my own temptation to get on the big speaking and writing circuits. I thank God and Pamela I did not get caught up in that."

The talk of success and survival gets Reuben thinking about King Herod. He threw a big dinner party, desperately trying to impress his peers, and after seeing Salome dance, right then and there he said, **Ask me for whatever you wish and I will grant it.** She said, **Give me at once the head of John the Baptist** (Mark 6:22, 25). Herod could not afford to lose face in the presence of his peers. Survival was too important.

Then Reuben thinks about Jesus' encounter with a rich, young ruler to whom He said, **Sell what you have, and give [it] to the poor** (Mark 10:21). The ruler said, "I can't," and Jesus said, "Yes, you can—it isn't all that bad after you've done it." "No, I can't. I have to survive."

"The key word here is 'I,'" Reuben says. "As in 'I must survive.' Actually, we don't need to survive. When we lay aside ourselves and take on the nature of God through Christ, we really don't need to survive anymore. That's the beauty of it."

Think about Caiaphas. For the nation to survive, Jesus has to go. And He did. And they did. Sort of. (See John 11:49-51.)

Or think about Pilate, calling for a bowl of water to wash his hands of Jesus, because Pilate was a survivor. (See Matt. 27:24.)

True to form, Reuben takes it out of the historical or hypothetical and applies it to where we live.

"What if we as a church, a college, a denomination, as a country, as a company and a business decided we just simply didn't need to survive anymore—that all we wanted to do was to do justice and to love mercy and walk humbly with our God? [See Mic. 6:8.]

"What if we gave up on competition and worked on doing the will of the Father, like feeding and clothing and cleaning up the slums, and educating and training?"

Success and survival were not the ultimate issue with Jesus in the wilderness, and they are not our true issue, either.

"God said to the Israelites, 'I didn't call you because you were good, or big, or better, or stronger, or nicer, or more religious, or more loyal, or less rebellious than anybody else, but I have set My love upon you. I have called you.'"

What Jesus did in the wilderness freed us from having to fit the contemporary models of our culture, where we evaluate ourselves by our peers, concluding that we are either superior or inferior.

"The thing that keeps coming back to my head again and again is if we have to survive, then survival is the issue," he says. "But if we could ever settle that issue and be free, then we could be free to love even if it doesn't pay. It wouldn't have to be cost-effective. Wouldn't it be a blessing if we could just give until we ran out, and that would be that? Is that all right? Of course not. Yes, it is. It really is."

What is uniquely Reuben about all of this is his ability not only to connect Jesus' temptation and victory to ours today but also to connect it all the way back to the beginning.

"The fundamental rule to survival is very much like original sin," he says. "It is the will to do what I want to do and to bring God down to work within it and bless it and use it. What if the will to survive is the fundamental sin? What if we could give our ego up to the Cross?"

When Jesus came out of the wilderness, knowing who He was and what He was called to do, the rest of His life was in obedience to His Father where He was free to show marvelous power, authority, and integrity.

"The rub is that He didn't survive," Reuben says. "But He lived His whole life in trust and commitment to His Father all the way to death, and He never backed out, or backed around, or worked it out, or made a deal because He settled the fundamental issue. And He did not survive. But He triumphed!

"There is something in me that rises with incredible joy and anticipation when I think of the freedom that comes when you don't have to survive. It's not passiveness. It's not inactivity. It's *becoming* who we are in Christ."

As you read Reuben's insights on the temptations of Jesus, remember that they may cause you to look at yourself with a new type of scrutiny. They are designed to set you free from having to "measure up" and "succeed."

I think one of the reasons I resigned from my position in Detroit after hearing these talks has to do with this very issue. As I look back, I consider it my own "wilderness" experience, where I struggled with who I was, whose I was, and what God's call was on my life. With the help of Reuben's talks on the temptations of Jesus and the relentless desire of Jesus to set me free from myself, I moved into a new level of obedience to the Father. As you read the following pages, I suspect you will too.

Then the devil took him to the holy city, and set him on the pinnacle of the temple, and said to him, "If you are the Son of God, throw yourself down; for it is written, 'He will give his angels charge of you,' and 'On their hands they will bear you up, lest you strike your foot against a stone.'" Jesus said to him, "Again it is written, 'You shall not tempt the Lord your God'" (Matt. 4:5-7).

Manipulating God

I believe that the temptations of Jesus were not endured just for our benefit. They were His own. Let me run that by again. *The temptations of Jesus were not for our benefit.* That does not mean, of course, that we do not profit from them. But He was not tempted on our behalf. The temptation experience was His. And the struggle was His.

He was not role-playing or playacting. He was not saying to himself, *Those who follow Me will be tempted, so I'd best be doing this so they will know how to act.* I think many have the feeling that Jesus went through these experiences as our Great Example, as our Pattern, so that we will understand how to resist the tempter in our time of trial. Of course, He does become a pattern for our lives, *after the fact.*

But the life He lived, the testings He experienced,

the hungers, the yearnings, the trials, and the obedience were all His. I believe that it is precisely because the temptation was *His* struggle, *His* battle, *His* own inner life test that it becomes so helpful for us.

But there is not a one-to-one ratio between His temptations and ours. We know He was tempted in all points as we are. That is true. But in another sense it is not true. He did not experience the temptations of a middle-aged married man of the 20th century. He did not experience the temptations of a single woman of college age. *Do you know what I mean?* But He did experience all that it means to be totally human and be tempted in all the ways humans are tempted. He entered totally into our human situation. The life He lived *was His own.* The faith that He had in His Father *was His own.* That is why He knows me so well and shares my struggles from inside.

I have been wondering how in the world it could have been any valid temptation for Jesus to leap off the pinnacle of the Temple.

Most of us are familiar with Jesus' temptation to turn stones into bread. What I really want to talk about is the temptation—His own real temptation—to leap off the pinnacle of the Temple. **Then the devil took him to the holy city, and set him on the pinnacle of the temple, and said to him, "If you are the Son of God, throw yourself down; for it is written, 'He will give his angels charge of you,' and 'On their hands they will bear you up, lest you strike your foot against a stone.'" Jesus** said to him, "Again it is written, 'You shall not tempt the Lord your God'" (Matt. 4:5-7).

I have been wondering how in the world it could have been any valid temptation for Jesus to leap off the pinnacle of the Temple. You know, of all the temptations I have ever had, *that has not been one of them!* How could it be a temptation to Jesus?

Maybe it will help to view it in light of contemporary Jewish messianic expectation. Jesus emerged from the waters of Jordan aware of His unique relationship to God, aware that the task to which He had been called was the task of messianic, suffering love. But we know, also, that He did not live in a vacuum. There were contemporary messianic expectations. We know that Satan quoted from Ps. 91:11-12. Let's just go back and read it: **For he will give his angels charge of you to guard you in all your ways. On their hands they will bear you up, lest you dash your foot against a stone.** Then it goes on to say: **You will tread on the lion and the adder, the young lion and the serpent you will trample under foot. Because he cleaves to me in love, I will deliver him; I will protect him, because he knows my name. When he calls to me, I will answer him; I will be with him in trouble, I will rescue him and honor him. With long life I will satisfy him, and show him my salvation** (vv. 13-16).

The scholars of Jesus' day looked at this psalm as a messianic psalm referring to the Anointed One who would come in the latter days. One of their commentaries says, "When King Messiah is revealed, He comes and stands upon the roof of the holy place. Then He will announce to the Israelites and say, 'Ye poor, the time of your redemption has come.'"

Let's step back and take a look at this. It is time

for the morning sacrifice. Worshipers are gathering in the courtyard, filled with expectation. Suddenly, appearing from the Temple pinnacle comes the Man from heaven. Surrounded by His angels, He descends into the midst of His worshiping followers. Their dreams have come true. Their prayers have been answered; the Messiah has come. I tell you, they will rise up and follow Him forever. *Well, at least until tomorrow.*

I have read that the masses are hungry for miracle, for mystery, for authority—and I believe it. They are hungry for gurus who have charisma, who have authority, who can reveal mystery, who can do magic. One of the temptations of Jesus was to feed this hunger, to accomplish His Father's purpose by catering to this desire for miracle, for mystery, and for authority.

In the young among whom I am privileged to live, there is a profound desire for a Christian life that is out of this world—fantastic something—out of the ordinary. There is a fundamental resistance to day-by-day, ordinary do your homework, eat right, go to bed, be nice kind of religion. *Now, that's true, isn't it? That's dull. It has no basic appeal.* What they want is a miracle.

Several years ago, I knew a man who claimed a gift of healing. People gathered at his house to get their legs equalized. I don't know what genetic problem caused it, but an astonishing number found out that one leg was shorter than the other. This man had a tremendous ability to lengthen the short leg!

One of the young fellows at school was all caught up in this. He had been to a meeting and found that one leg was just about two inches shorter than the other. They put him in a chair, put his legs out, the healer prayed, and that short leg came right out, and he was OK. We were at a student/faculty committee meeting when this student came in and shared the exciting news of his lengthened leg. I never will forget the president's response—no change of expression—*"Well, for goodness' sake. Isn't that interesting."* And we went on with the meeting.

I've had a special liking for him ever since. He had the ability to say, *"Hmm. Ain't it a wonder."* He didn't give *too* much credence to this display of healing power. Why didn't he? I believe it was because the miracle was obviously sensational. Its end was not discipleship but amazement.

For that matter, I have not been able to recover from what happened in Jonestown, Guyana. I keep thinking of the normal, ordinary, good people who hungered for peace and security. They wanted affirmation. They wanted love. They had real, deep, genuine needs, and they found someone who loved them like nobody else, who had authority and charisma. And they sold their freedom for the miraculous, for the mysterious, for the authoritarian, and they followed him all the way to death. *I cannot get that out of my head.* And when you think of how many people are capitalizing on the hunger for the miraculous . . .

Out our way, we have a TV preacher. I've heard more about him than I've seen him. He has people come up to be healed, or "slain in the Spirit." His white-suited cohorts are standing around and he stretches out his hand and the people fall down, just laid out in the Lord, slain in the Spirit. *Ain't it a wonder?*

And I wonder whose real needs are being met? For whose glory is the performance? What do the miracles mean? It helps me to know that Jesus faced these very issues. He had to answer the questions, "All right, who am I? How am I going to fulfill My ministry?"

We know about healers. We know about sensational leaders who say, "You've got to get the attention of the world. You've got to have a miracle or what looks like one. This is what folks want. Give them what they want." But Jesus turned away from those expectations and took the lonely path to Calvary's cross to die. *Once in a while I remember that, and when I do, it scares me a little.*

There's another dimension to this temptation that I think is even more fundamental. I believe that Jesus interpreted the meaning of the temptation by the way He answered the tempter. Again, it is the temptation to test the validity of His relationship with His Father. It is as though Satan said to Him something like this: "If You are the Son of God, then You have a claim on God. Whatever happens, You will be saved from harm." And in order to test and show that God was present with Him, Jesus was tempted to put His Father in a position that would make it necessary for Him to respond to the trustful act of Jesus. He was tempted to *use* His Father, to manipulate Him in order to prove that He was the Father's Son. Jesus understood the temptation that way. He quoted from Deuteronomy: **You shall not put the LORD your God to the test, as you tested him at Massah. You shall diligently keep the commandments of the LORD your God, and his testimonies, and his statutes, which he has commanded you. And you shall do what is right and good in sight of the LORD** (6:16-18).

Did you hear that? **You shall not put the LORD your God to the test, as you tested him at Massah.** The Massah incident comes out of Exod. 17:

All the congregation of the people of Israel moved on from the wilderness . . . and camped at Rephidim; but there

was no water for the people to drink. Therefore the people found fault with Moses, and said, "Give us water to drink." And Moses said to them, "Why do you find fault with me? Why do you put the LORD to the proof?" But the people thirsted there for water, and the people murmured against Moses, and said, "Why did you bring us up out of Egypt, to kill us and our children and our cattle with thirst?" So Moses cried to the LORD, "What shall I do with this people? They are almost ready to stone me." And the LORD said to Moses, ". . . Behold, I will stand before you there on the rock at Horeb; and you shall strike the rock, and water shall come out of it, that the people may drink." . . . And he called the name of the place Massah and Meribah, because of the faultfinding of the children of Israel.

Listen to this:

And because they put the LORD to the proof by saying, "Is the LORD among us or not?" (vv. 1-7).

What a question! Is the Lord among us, or not?

Have you ever noticed that most of what the Holy Spirit is doing is where somebody else is? **It's discouraging, isn't it?** *And over here where we are, things aren't quite so exciting.*

Am I a child of God, or not? Given our Western way of thinking, the conclusion is natural: How can you prove you are a child of God? And we get an "if-then" syndrome going; it goes like this: *If* the Lord is among us and we really have the Holy Spirit, *then a-b-c-d-e* will follow. But maybe we are not seeing *a-b-c-d-e*. *Where is God?* Over there some superchurch is going gung ho, and over here where we are—nothing!

Have you ever noticed that most of what the Holy Spirit is doing is where somebody else is? *It's discouraging, isn't it?* And over here where we are, things aren't quite so exciting. *Is God with us, or not? Is He with us? What's the matter with us?* And when we are at that point, we are terribly vulnerable. Our church (I think I'll just say *our church* with a small *c*, and that includes the whole bunch of us), our church doesn't seem to be growing all that much, and some other parts of the Kingdom are spreading like wildfire, and we are wondering what has gone wrong. We are at a most dangerous and vulnerable place, *aren't we?*

Right at this point, we begin to ask questions: Where is the glory of the bygone day? Where is God working? Are we His children? What needs to be happening to demonstrate that God is indeed among us? We are tempted to fulfill expectation, to cater to miracle, to mystery, to authority. One way or another, we've got to demonstrate our status with God. And underneath is the question hidden and unspoken: *Is God with us, or not?*

Now, the worst of this temptation is that it is done with Scripture and it takes place in the Temple of God. *Think about that a minute.* Where is the great inner strength of Jesus about himself and His task? It's in the Scripture and it's in the Temple of God. And Scripture is used by both Satan and Jesus.

The first temptation was **Command these stones**

to become . . . bread. Satan didn't back it up with Scripture, but Jesus answered him, **It is written . . .** (Matt. 4:3-4). Satan picks up on that and says, "All right, then do this . . . because it is written . . ." Jesus answered, "No! because it is written . . ." SATAN USED SCRIPTURE AGAINST JESUS, AND JESUS USED SCRIPTURE AGAINST SATAN, *and sometimes that's a little scary.*

Here is the crucial difference: Satan *used* Scripture; Jesus trusted His Father and lived under the authority of Scripture in obedience to His Father's Word. In one sense, if Jesus had leaped from the Temple, He would have been doing it as an act of trust in His Father's promise. He could have leaped singing, "Standing on the promises of God!"

Well, let's look back at Ps. 91:11-12: **He will give his angels charge of you . . . On their hands they will bear you up, lest you dash your foot against a stone.** *Is that true or false?* **He will . . . guard you in all your ways.** *Is that true or false? Is God's Word the Truth?* And if His Word is the Truth and we are His people and we trust His promise, then we can say, "Take God at His Word, and step out on His promises."

Well, is the Word of God true or false? It is true, of course.

Listen to some scriptures: **Bring ye all the tithes into the storehouse . . . and prove me now herewith, saith the LORD of hosts, if I will not open you the windows of heaven, and pour you out a blessing, that there shall not be room enough to receive it** (Mal. 3:10, KJV). And other such good things in the passage as are added by the pastor when the offerings are down.

Well, is that promise true or false? Does God keep His Word? It matters terribly how we answer these questions and how we respond to the promise.

One thing we can do and have done is step out on
the promise in obedience and look for riches and
blessings to follow. Do you remember a brother who
not too long ago was ministering among us saying,
"What we need to do is tithe on the amount of in-
come we want to receive. God loves Cadillacs. How
much money do you want? Start tithing on that
amount—you can't lose."

Here's the premise: God keeps His Word. What is
His Word? It is spiritual law. Tithe, and you will receive. **Give, and it will be given to you** (Luke
6:38). Do you want to be given unto? Then, give. God
honors His Word. He loves to keep His Word. He loves
for His people to step out on His Word.

Oh, I can hear the TV preachers now, can't you? I
can hear a few un-TV preachers too. *So keep those
cards and letters coming in, folks, and we'll keep
this program on the air and have a worldwide ministry, and I'll send you a free copy of my book by re-
turn mail.* Well, does God keep His Word or not?
**Train up a child in the way he should go: and
when he is old, he will not depart from it** (Prov.
22:6, KJV).

Is that true? All right, then, discipline and trust
God. You will have the model family. *Does the Bible
mean what it says, or doesn't it? Is God true to His
promise, or not?* Step out on the promise. Act and
God will come through.

You know what this sounds like? *If* you do your
part, *then* God is obligated to do His part. He has
promised and He will fulfill. *If* you act, *then* He will respond. *I hope we get out of this all right, don't you?
Hang on! If* you take Him at His word, *if* you believe
and not doubt, you have pulled the levers that activate
the power of God. He will come through for you.

And Jesus said, **You shall not tempt the Lord**

your God (Matt. 4:7). I remember talking to a pastor friend of mine who went through a time of darkness and despair. He had no sense of God. I mean, God was nowhere. *And if you do not understand that, just tune out.* Have you ever had those times when nothing speaks to you in a book you have, and there's not a verse in the Bible that helps? There's just nothing, nowhere. He was in one of those times. And he said, "I'm going into my study, and I'm not coming out until I know God is real."

He went into his study, locked the door, cut off the phone, and began to pray, *and nothing happened.* So he prayed some more, crying in distress, "God, if You are real and I am Your child, then let a breeze blow, let a piece of paper fall, let something—anything—happen so I'll know. I'm not leaving here until I know. O God, do something." You know the result of that. Nothing happened. No papers gently shifted off the desk. No cobweb swayed from the ceiling. Nothing.

> *Do you know that with all the clout and power Jesus had,* **He lived all His life in obedience and trust in His Father, and He never put His Father to the test.**

Finally, when he was too tired to pray anymore, he relaxed. He suddenly saw himself and what he was doing and began to laugh—and he was OK. Do you see what he was doing? The same thing we do. He was manipulating God, forcing an answer to the question *Is God with me, or not?*

Folks, do you know that with all the clout and

power Jesus had, *He lived all His life in obedience and trust in His Father, and He never put His Father to the test.* He went all the way to Calvary, and He could have called ten thousand angels. *Just think about that.* I think this is the significant element in the temptation because Jesus quoted this scripture in answer to the tempter: **You shall not put the LORD your God to the test, as you tested him at Massah** (Deut. 6:16).

What was the Massah temptation? **Is the LORD among us or not?** (Exod. 17:7). The if-then syndrome: *If* you are the Son of God, *then* ... put God to the test. And Jesus lived His life in good times and bad times, in affirmation times and denial times, in high times and low times, in fasting and feasting, in acceptance and rejection. *He lived His life trusting His Father,* as the scripture said in Deuteronomy: **diligently keep[ing] the commandments of the LORD . . . and do[ing] what is right and good in the sight of the LORD** (6:17-18). And not saying, **Is the LORD among us or not?** *That helps me!*

And what I hear out of this passage is: *Do not say,* "Is the Lord among us or not?" *Do not say,* "Is God with me?" Don't say that. Obey God. Trust God. Do what is right and good in the sight of the Lord. Don't ask for something to demonstrate that He is with you. Believe it: He is with you.

I understand the hunger for magic, for miracle, for mystery, for authority. But Jesus never put His Father to the test. **You shall not tempt the Lord your God.** Do you see what it does to God when we put Him to the test? "If you will—then God will." It makes God into an impersonal power and makes no reference to His holy, personal will. "If you do your part, then God is obligated to do His."

When I hear that, something rises up inside me

to say, *Oh, wait a minute! Who is who in this business?* Sometimes I see a little slogan posted around that says, Expect a Miracle! If you have those posters in your church, I hope you will still love me and understand that I'd like you to go and take them down and try not to ruin the paint. Expect a miracle! Expect a miracle? Not if it creates a demand that divine power respond to your command. Not if it makes faith a lever to manipulate divine activity.

At a time when our college leader was seriously ill and failing, students began to rally and to say, We can't have this. We need him. We have got to bind together, trust God, *and get him healed.* Do you understand that? God can get glory out of this, *and we have to get him healed.* Let's bind together. Let's get a prayer chain. Let's get hold of God *and get him healed.*

> ## *Our faith is not dependent upon the miraculous work of God to demonstrate that He is among us.*

I did a lot of thinking in those days about such things. I think that is partly what has brought about these thoughts and probings in my own heart about this temptation of Jesus. You see, if God is with us and we believe, *then God will heal.* Claim His promise, step out on His promise, *then God will act.*

What's hard is, I believe all that. BUT WHEN IT BECOMES A MANIPULATION OF GOD, WE ARE PUTTING HIM TO THE TEST. And I will tell you what I came to believe during those days: If the college leader is healed, Jesus is Lord! If our school flourishes, Jesus is Lord! If it declines, Jesus is Lord! If our church grows, Jesus is Lord! If it does not grow, Jesus is Lord!

He is in charge here. And our faith is not dependent upon the miraculous work of God to demonstrate that He is among us. So I want you to get another poster to put up in place of the one you took down: Don't Expect a Miracle!

Our oldest daughter is brain-damaged, mentally challenged, and institutionalized. And we've gone the route of expecting miracles. We've gone the route of healing services and anointings. You name it; we've done it. And nothing has happened, *and Jesus is Lord!*

I know people all around the place who want a miracle, and I think it can be a cop-out. Don't expect a miracle. Obey God! **You shall not put the LORD your God to the test.** Don't expect a miracle, *but keep the commandments of the Lord and do what is right in the sight of the Lord.* I believe that this is precisely the kind of faith Jesus had. I believe it is the kind of faith that trusts the Father to do His gracious will, with or without miracles. It is faith that trusts and believes and does not manipulate. He is in charge here.

We may trust Him; we may not manipulate Him.

> *Trusting as the moments fly;*
> *Trusting as the days go by;*
> *Trusting Him whate'er befall;*
> *Trusting Jesus, that is all.*
> —Edgar Page Stites

Systems and Compromises

The hard part of all this is that we *do* live in this world and we *do* make compromises. There are traditions and feelings and systems to deal with. There are things that happen that we do not like that seem to be inevitable.

But here's what I am thinking: *Aren't you glad*

that someone has come and lived among us who was not a pragmatist, who didn't ever compromise, and who did not seek to build the kingdom of God by capitulating to the system of the world, who did not do the Father's will by working wisely with the status quo? I have to say, *Thank God,* the body politic is not eternal! The chain of inevitability has been broken. Into our world, fast bound by its systems and its fallenness, has come One who walked with His heart open to the Father, who paid the full price of total obedience, who never did sell out to the system. *Now that means something for me.*

I know that I must live in the compromises and tensions between the value structure of the Kingdom and the value structure of the world, but I tell you, I know what God's will is for us in this world. Jesus has lived it out. I can bring to Him *in repentance* the failures, the compromises of my life as I live and work within the fallen system of the world—the world He came to redeem.

This is the tension in which we live, and which can only be resolved by the spirit of repentance. I THINK THE GREAT TEMPTATION WE HAVE IS TO DILUTE THE COMMANDS OF GOD, to water down the demands of the Kingdom in such a way that we can live with them in peace. While, in fact, we are capitulating to the fallen systems of the world. But in our humanness and in our weakness, there is open to us the way of repentance and confession, of openness to the God of all grace whose Spirit is faithful to check, to reprove, to instruct as we seek to find God's way in this world.

Our faith is that the gospel is greater than the ancient inveterate powers of evil. The system is not ultimate. God's grace is operative within it. It's obvious that I don't have answers to this tension. The problems can't be solved by saying, You can do this, and you can't that. This is OK in the Kingdom, but that won't do. What the Lord is saying to me is this: I HAVE TO KEEP THAT SYSTEM EXPOSED TO THE JUDGMENT OF GOD AND LIVE IN A SPIRIT OF HU-MILITY AND REPENTANCE that won't let me function with complacency, pride, coldness of heart, and self-righteousness while the system does its work.

At the same time, I need to be fully aware that the grace and the mercy and the power of God are at work through our world to redeem and to save. *Oh, I believe that, don't you?* You know, and so do I, that there have been people who have been hurt by good systems, and it has turned out to be God's gracious, beautiful providence in their lives. *I believe that.* I don't see any way to be naive. Our institutional world is a part of the fallenness of the total scheme of things. But I can't get away from the fact that into the cycle of inevitability our pure, honest, obedient Lord Jesus has come and broken the chains. God raised Him from the dead and laid out before us His pattern, His lifestyle. I go on living in the system and go on attending the meetings that go on dealing with the problems that call for compromise and expediency and fiscal responsibility.

What is God's will for me? It is to work in that system redeemingly, lovingly, sufferingly, caringly, willing to expose that whole system to God's verdict in repentance. It is to know that in and through the whole thing the loving, caring power of God is at work. Because, you see, it is precisely into the world that Jesus has come. **God so loved the world . . .** *This world? With its fallenness? With its compromises? With its policies?* **God so loved the world** (John 3:16)!